Also by Margaret K. Hunter and Edgar H. Hunter:

The Indoor Garden: Design, Construction, and Furnishing

YOUR OWN KITCHEN AND GARDEN SURVIVAL BOOK

Margaret King Hunter and
Virginia W. Williams

Illustrated by Edgar H. Hunter

Simon and Schuster   New York

Special thanks to my aunt, Kathryn Greenough Hall, for her loving encouragement of this work.

Published by Simon and Schuster
A Division of Gulf & Western Corporation
Simon & Schuster Building
Rockefeller Center
1230 Avenue of the Americas
New York, New York 10020

Designed by Elizabeth Woll
Manufactured in the United States of America

1 2 3 4 5 6 7 8 9 10

Library of Congress Cataloging in Publication Data
Hunter, Margaret K., date.
    Your Own Kitchen and garden survival book.

Includes index.
    1. Cookery. 2. Vegetable gardening. 3. Organic gardening.
I. Williams, Virginia W., joint author. II. Title.
TX715.H923   641.5   78-1938
ISBN 0-671-22694-0
ISBN 0-671-24241-5 Pbk.

This book is dedicated to my mother, Margaret Greenough King, and my father, Talmage Damron King, who taught me all that was worth knowing—especially how to live; and to my husband, Edgar Hayes Hunter, a stalwart and courageous man—my pillar in adversity, my companion in joy.

MARGARET KING HUNTER

Contents

"The authors of this volume, while they sympathize with every honest effort to relieve the disabilities and sufferings of their sex, are confident that the chief cause of these evils is the fact that the honor and duties of the family state are not duly appreciated, that women are not trained for these duties as men are trained for their trades and professions and that, as the consequence, family labor is poorly done, poorly paid and regarded as menial and disgraceful.

"To be the nurse of young children, a cook and a housemaid is regarded as the lowest and last resort of poverty, and one which no woman of culture and position can assume without loss of caste and respectability.

"There are but a few things on which health and happiness depend, more than on the manner in which food is cooked. You may make houses enchantingly beautiful, hang them with pictures, have them clean and airy and convenient; but if the stomach is fed with sour bread and burnt meats, it will raise such rebellions that the eyes will see no beauty anywhere. The abundance of splendid material we have in America is in great contrast with the style of cooking most prevalent in our country.

"Considering that our resources are greater than those of any civilized people, our results are comparatively poorer." (From Catharine Beecher and Harriet Beecher Stowe, The American Woman's Home [New York: J. B. Ford & Co., 1869].) Reprinted by Arno Press, Inc., 1972.

Preface

We have called this Your Own Kitchen and Garden Survival Book since it is not only a cookbook which includes special homemaking tips, but also because it includes some "how-tos" for home vegetable gardening. Peg has always used her vegetable garden as an adjunct to her kitchen and has found it impossible to separate the two in writing this book.

Eating is not merely for nourishment any more than gardening is only for growing food. Each is accompanied by rewarding pleasures which add to the rich pattern of life. While cooking, think of eating not only for good health, but to savor various flavors and textures, the bland and soft with the sharp and crisp, the salty with the sweet, the bitter with the sweet, the crunchy with the mushy, etc. Use your imagination and don't be afraid to try new things.

The dollars saved by the economies suggested here are almost tax-free dollars. When you earn a dollar, it is taxed when you receive it and also taxed when you spend it. No one has yet found out how to tax household economies at the source. You will, in this case, only be taxed when you spend your savings. Think of dollars saved as worth fifty percent more than dollars earned, and you will try to put into practice every economy which you can apply to your circumstances.

As we have worked on this book, we have realized that we are trying to provide a sort of bridge from total supermarket dependency to total natural, organic living. We feel that this job has needed to be done, since, for most suburban or city dwellers, pure "organic" living is difficult, if not almost impossible at this time, or all at once. However, as you use this book and become more used to thinking economy and ecology, you will find ways opening to cross the bridge which we hope we have made.

BREADS

OUR BLUE RIBBON TIP

During World War II, ration books and scarcities produced this money-saving and healthful recipe for using gelatin to extend butter or margarine.

4 teaspoons unflavored gelatin	1 teaspoon salt
1 pound butter	1 cup milk

Sprinkle gelatin over cold milk in saucepan. Place over low heat, stirring constantly until gelatin dissolves. Remove from heat, add salt and cool to room temperature.

Cut butter into small pieces and heat over hot water until soft enough to beat. Do not melt butter. Gradually whip milk into butter with mixer until milk is entirely absorbed. Pack into container and refrigerate until hard. Use on vegetables, pancakes, waffles, rolls, bread, bread puddings. Do not use for frying, sautéing, or greasing pans. Another even less expensive spread would be to use ½ margarine and ½ butter or all margarine. For a large party, buy two butter paddles at a gourmet shop and make large, marble-sized balls for serving with rolls, or buy an attractive butter mold to pack this spread. Unmold and serve for a party. An ice-cream scoop of our "butter" makes a nice table serving. We do 3 pounds at a time. Pack in freezer boxes and freeze butter for use as needed. Watch for butter or margarine sales for this purpose.

QUICK-RISE BREAD (Two Loaves)

5 ½ to 6 ½ cups all-purpose flour
  2 packages dry yeast
  2 tablespoons sugar

  1 tablespoon salt
2 ¼ cups hot tap water
    Salad oil

Combine 2 cups flour, undissolved yeast, sugar and salt in a large bowl, stirring well to blend. Add hot tap water to ingredients in bowl all at once. Beat 2 minutes with electric mixer at medium speed. Scrape sides of bowl occasionally. Add 1 cup more of flour. Beat 1 minute with electric mixer at high speed, or until thick and elastic. Scrape sides of bowl occasionally. Stir in enough of remaining flour to make a soft dough that leaves the sides of the bowl. Turn onto floured board. Round up into ball. Knead 5 to 10 minutes or until smooth and elastic. Cover with plastic wrap and a towel. Let rest on board 20 minutes.

Punch down. Divide dough into 2 equal parts. Roll each portion into an 8-inch by 12-inch rectangle. Roll up tightly into loaves at 8-inch side. Seal lengthwise edge, and ends, well. Tuck ends under. Place in greased loaf pans. Brush surface of dough with salad oil. Cover pans loosely with waxed paper. Refrigerate 2 to 24 hours. When ready to bake, remove from refrigerator, uncover. Let stand 10 minutes. Preheat oven to 375°, bake for 10 minutes, then lower temperature to 350°. Bake 25 to 30 minutes more. Remove from pans and cool on racks. Brush with water while hot if you want a crisp crust, with butter or margarine if a soft crust is wanted.

Tip

When using bulk yeast: 1 tablespoon = 1 package dry yeast.

QUICK-RISE BREAD VARIATIONS

RYE OR WHOLE WHEAT BREAD

2½ cups rye or whole wheat flour   3 to 4 cups white flour

Wheat germ can be added. Just be sure that the total amount of flour is 5½ to 6½ cups. A nice change is to use 1 cup cornmeal. You can make loaves of French bread, also. Bake on a greased cookie sheet. Homemade hamburger rolls and hot dog rolls are a real treat.

Tip

Do you know that by making the quick-rise bread recipe in 3 separate batches (a multiplied recipe mixed together is seldom a success) and baking 6 loaves at a time, you can bake your week's bread supply in the same time and with the same amount of fuel which you would use to heat a TV dinner?

Tip

When measuring solid shortening to get a correct measure, if your recipe calls for ½ cup shortening, fill measuring cup half full of cold water, then add shortening until water comes to top of cup. Pour off water and go ahead with your recipe.

WHOLE WHEAT ONION BUNS

1 tablespoon butter
¼ cup chopped onions
3 cups white flour
3 cups whole wheat flour

3 tablespoons sugar
1½ teaspoons salt
2 packages yeast
2 cups hot water

In a small pan, sauté onions in butter slowly until golden, about 7 minutes. In large bowl, blend together 1 cup white flour, 1 cup whole wheat flour, sugar, salt, and yeast. Reserve 2 tablespoons of the onion-butter. Mix remaining onion and butter into yeast mixture. Pour in the hot water.

Add 1 more cup of whole wheat flour and beat at high speed with the electric mixer for 2 minutes. Stir in the remaining 1 cup of whole wheat flour to make a soft dough. Sprinkle the board with flour and knead until smooth and elastic, about 5 minutes. Place in a greased bowl, cover, and let rise until double in bulk (about 1 hour).

Punch down and divide dough into 20 pieces. Roll into balls and place on greased cookie sheets. With greased fingers, flatten each ball into a 4-inch circle. Spread about ¼ teaspoon of reserved onions on top of each circle.

Cover and let rise until double, about 50 minutes. Bake in a 375° oven for 20 to 25 minutes or until brown. Makes 20 rolls. These are excellent used as hamburger rolls.

DELICATE ROLLS

1 package yeast	4 tablespoons sugar
1 cup lukewarm water	6 tablespoons solid shortening
1 teaspoon sugar	1 egg, beaten
1 cup scalded milk	5 to 6 cups presifted flour
2 teaspoons salt	

Pour yeast into lukewarm water; add 1 teaspoon sugar and stir; let stand 5 minutes. Pour scalded milk into mixing bowl, add salt, sugar, shortening; let cool to lukewarm. Add yeast, two cups of flour, and the egg. Beat smooth with electric beater. Add remaining flour a cup at a time, mixing with spoon until each cupful is thoroughly mixed in. Use your judgment about whether or not to add that sixth cupful, since you want a dough softer than bread dough. Knead on a floured cloth or board until smooth and elastic. Grease a bowl with butter heavily, and place ball of dough in it. Brush top with a little melted butter, cover with waxed paper or plastic to prevent drying out. Let rise until double in bulk. (If the room is cold, turn oven to lowest setting; turn it on and then off after a minute. Place bowl in oven; leave oven door open for 1 minute; close gently). Check on your dough after an hour. When dough has doubled in bulk, punch down and let rise to double again. Shape into large egg-sized rolls and place in greased 9-inch by 9-inch pans about ½ inch apart. Let rise to double again then bake for 15 to 20 minutes in 375⁰ oven.

FLORENCE CUTTING'S POPOVERS

2 eggs   1 cup sifted flour
1 cup milk   ½ teaspoon salt

Break eggs into bowl. Add milk, flour, and salt. Mix well with spoon. Disregard lumps. Fill well-greased muffin tins ¾ full. <u>Starting with cold oven,</u> bake at setting of 450⁰ for 25 minutes. Do not open oven for 25 minutes. Makes 9.

THE KING'S ENGLISH MUFFINS

1 package yeast
¼ cup lukewarm water
1 cup milk
2 tablespoons sugar
1½ teaspoons salt

3 tablespoons shortening
4 cups flour (about)
1 egg
    About 2 tablespoons cornmeal

Dissolve yeast in lukewarm water. Scald milk and add sugar, salt, and shortening. Cool to lukewarm. Add 2 cups flour. Mix well. Add dissolved yeast and egg. Beat thoroughly. Add enough more flour to make moderately soft dough (about 2 cups). Turn out on lightly floured board and knead until smooth and satiny. Put in greased bowl. Grease surface lightly. Cover and let rise in warm place until doubled (about 1 hour). Punch down and let rest 10 minutes. Roll out ¼ inch thick. Cut with 3-inch cookie cutter. Place on cookie sheet on which cornmeal has been sprinkled.

Cover and let rise until doubled in size (about 45 minutes). Bake slowly on ungreased heavy griddle or fry pan.

Have griddle hot at first, then reduce heat to brown muffins slowly. Bake 6 to 8 minutes on each side. (Sometimes takes less than that, but the slower cooking makes the better muffins.) Yield about 12 3-inch muffins.

PEG'S MOTHER'S CRANBERRY BREAD (via Virginia)

2 cups sifted all-purpose flour
1 cup sugar
1½ teaspoons baking powder
1 teaspoon salt
¼ cup vegetable oil
1 teaspoon grated orange peel

¾ cup orange juice
1 egg, beaten
1 cup fresh cranberries, coarsely chopped
½ cup nut meats, chopped

Sift together flour, sugar, baking powder, and salt. Combine vegetable oil, orange peel, orange juice, and egg. Add to dry ingredients, mixing just to moisten. Fold in cranberries and nuts. Turn into a greased 9-inch by 5-inch by 3-inch bread pan. Bake in oven at 350° for 60 minutes. Cool—do not cut until next day.

Mrs. King delighted in making the cranberry bread at Christmastime and mailing a loaf to each of her four daughters and giving it away to friends. We kept some in the freezer to use with tea, toasted and buttered.

Tip

To save on butter or margarine at mealtime, cut in slices of 1 tablespoon for each person at the table.

CHALLAH — BRAIDED BREAD

½ teaspoon salt
1 tablespoon sugar
1 tablespoon salad oil
1½ cups hot water
1 package yeast

1 egg
5 to 6 cups unsifted flour
1 egg yolk
1 tablespoon water
1 teaspoon sesame seeds

Put salt, sugar, and oil in a large bowl; pour hot water over the ingredients and stir until the sugar is dissolved. Cool to lukewarm and add yeast, stirring until dissolved. Add egg. With a spoon, mix in 4½ cups flour to form dough. Coat board with ½ cup flour and knead until smooth and elastic (about 5 minutes). Add more flour if needed.

Place in a greased bowl, cover, and let rise until double (1½ hours). Punch down and divide into 4 equal parts; roll to form strands 21 inches long. Place the 4 strips lengthwise on greased cookie sheet and braid. Tuck ends under and seal. Take yolk of egg and combine with 1 tablespoon water; with pastry brush, brush evenly over bread. Sprinkle with sesame seeds. Cover and let rise until double, about 1 hour. Bake at 350° for 30 to 35 minutes or until wooden toothpick comes out clean.

BEST DUMPLINGS EVER

2 cups sifted flour
3 teaspoons baking powder
1 teaspoon salt
½ teaspoon basil

¼ cup vegetable oil
1 cup milk
1 medium onion, grated

Sift flour, baking powder, salt, and basil into a bowl. Add all at once vegetable oil, milk, and grated onion. Stir as little as possible, using a fork. Drop by teaspoonful on top of chicken fricassee, stew, or soup. (Dip spoon in water, then in dough, and dumpling will drop right off spoon into the pot.) Simmer 10 minutes uncovered and turn dumplings over; cover tightly and simmer covered for 10 minutes more.

Tip

To keep dumplings nice and fluffy, keep pot covered. Here are some additions to brighten dumplings—your choice:

¼ cup parsley, chopped fine
2 tablespoons grated cheese
    Pinch thyme, marjoram

½ teaspoon finely chopped raw onion
3 tablespoons minced parsley and
    green sweet pepper, mixed

ROLLED OATS BREAD

½ cup boiling water
2 tablespoons shortening
4 cups rolled oats
1 cup sugar
1 tablespoon salt

1 yeast cake or 1 tablespoon
  powdered yeast
1 cup lukewarm water
1 cup cold water
4 cups white flour

Place boiling water and shortening in a large bowl; stir to melt shortening. Add rolled oats, sugar, salt, and stir together. When mixture is cool, dissolve the yeast in lukewarm water, then add cold water. Add yeast to oats and shortening. Sift 4 cups flour and stir into mixture. Turn out on board and knead 5 minutes. Put in greased bowl; let rise until double (about 1 hour). Turn onto board, make 2 round loaves, place on greased cookie sheet, and let rise again. Bake at 375° about 40 minutes. Cool on racks.

Tip
Any dish in which dough or egg has been prepared should be rinsed with cold water before being washed, as hot water tends to cook dough or egg, making it more difficult to remove.

GINGERBREAD MUFFINS

1 beaten egg
¾ cup melted margarine
1½ cups milk
½ cup molasses
2¾ cups flour
¼ cup white sugar

¼ cup brown sugar
1½ teaspoons soda
¾ teaspoon each, salt, cinnamon,
   and ginger
¼ teaspoon ground cloves

Mix first 4 ingredients together. Sift rest of ingredients. Combine them, mixing well. Fill muffin tins ¾ full. Bake at 350° for 25 minutes.

MELBA TOAST

Cut the thinnest possible slice of any kind of bread. Put on a cookie sheet and place in the oven at the lowest temperature; leave until it is light brown and crisp. To keep toast from curling, place second cookie sheet or cake rack on top of bread.

FRENCH BREAD

Combine

Measure into a large mixing bowl

1 envelope dry yeast
¼ cup lukewarm water
1 tablespoon sugar

4 cups flour
2 teaspoons salt
½ teaspoon sugar

Make a hole in the center of the dry mixture, pour into it the yeast mixture, and add 1⅓ cups lukewarm water. Stir thoroughly but do not knead. The dough will be soft. Cover with a damp tea towel and let it rise in a warm place, about 2 hours. Place on a lightly floured board and pat into two oblongs. Form into French loaf by rolling the dough, pressing outward with the hands and tapering toward the ends until a long, thin loaf is achieved. Place the 2 loaves on a greased cookie sheet; cut three diagonal slits across the top with scissors to form indentations.

Set in a warm place to rise to double in bulk. Bake 15 minutes at 400°, then lower heat to 350° and bake 30 minutes more. Immediately on taking from the oven, brush loaves with water. This ensures a crisp crust.

Tip

Soak a brick in water the night before making French Bread. Take brick from water and put it on the bottom shelf of the oven while bread is baking. You will have very crisp, beautiful loaves when bread is baked.

MEAT, FISH, FOWL, EGG, CHEESE

Tips

To use your time most efficiently, try taking a Saturday morning to cook for your freezer. It is such a help to have something ready when you are tired or have unexpected guests. Plan your use of cooking fuel in doing this.

When freezing ahead for daily use, try to package things in the measured amounts you usually need for your favorite recipes. This way you will not have more than you need. Less waste!

When using an electric stove, try to save the usually wasted extra heat in the coils. In cooking many foods, the stove can be turned all the way off before the end of the cooking time. The leftover heat, plus a little extra time, will produce a good result. You shouldn't pull the pan off the burner while it is still producing heat calories. That's waste!

PEG'S OYSTERS AND MUSHROOMS

1 quart fresh oysters (shucked)
1 pound sliced fresh mushrooms
2 small cans pimientos (or the
    equivalent of 2 of your own
    peppers made into pimientos)
4 tablespoons butter

8 tablespoons flour
1 cup milk
½ pint heavy cream
    Salt and pepper to taste

Simmer oysters in their liquor in a pan until their edges begin to curl. Set aside. Sauté mushrooms and pimientos slightly in butter. Mix flour with the milk and add to mushrooms, stirring well over low heat. When mixture begins to thicken, add cream, salt, and pepper; add oysters and their liquor. If it seems too thick, add more milk until of the right consistency. Serve over melba toast, brown rice, or a mixture of brown and wild rice. Oysters, mushrooms, and pimientos all have distinctive mild flavors; each should be detectable. The oysters should be dominant. We use this for a party dish, or buffet supper. Serves 10.

Tip

If you have "oyster cramp" from shucking oysters, try this: dip them in carbonated water; they will relax their resistance. If you have oyster-shucking cramp it is small wonder, because it takes an hour of continuous pulling equal to 22 pounds to tire the oyster into opening its shell.

JIM KING'S PAELLA

1 good-sized fryer-broiler chicken
1 medium-sized onion
1 clove garlic
  Olive oil
1 Spanish sausage, Portuguese
    linguica, or half a package of
    Smoky links
2 cups uncooked long-grain rice
4 cups chicken broth

½ teaspoon Spanish saffron
  Salt and pepper
6 or 8 clams in shell, or one # 2 can
1 cup peeled fresh shrimp, or one # 2
  can
1 large fresh tomato
1 large green pepper
½ cup green or ripe olives

    Cut up chicken; broil in oven, turning once, until nearly done and most of the fat is cooked out.

    Meanwhile, chop onion and garlic; fry lightly until transparent in a little olive oil in an electric frying pan (about 2 inches deep), which may be used as a serving dish. Add hot chicken pieces, drained of fat, from oven, mix with onion and garlic, and arrange in bottom of skillet.

    Add Spanish sausage cut up in bite-sized pieces. Fry gently with chicken till hot.

    Add uncooked rice. Work around among chicken pieces so it is evenly distributed. Continue frying gently till rice is hot.

    Meanwhile, prepare broth. (Chicken back and neck and gizzard may be simmered for broth. Also if you use canned clams and/or shrimp, liquor from shellfish may make part of 4 cups.) Bring to a simmer on stove and add Spanish saffron (very expensive, but a little goes a long way) so saffron will be evenly distributed in the dish. Add salt and pepper to taste.

Add hot broth to hot ingredients already in electric skillet and cover. Bring to boil and keep at simmer range until rice begins to cook. When rice is about half done, add clams in shell (hinges down at bottom of skillet, so they will open up facing upward) and shrimp, evenly distributed. If you use canned clams and canned shrimp (already cooked), add a little later. Arrange on top thin slices of tomato, green pepper (sweet pepper) rings, and olives.

Simmer with lid on until rice, tomato slices, and pepper rings on top are done. Serve.

Paella is like hash in that you can vary the ingredients somewhat, e.g., adding squid rings or crab. The essential idea is chicken and seafood cooked together with rice, and flavored with saffron.

BAKED WHOLE FISH

If you are fortunate enough to have a fisherman in the family, choose one or two 14- to 16-inch plump fish from the catch. Remove fins. Reach in and pull out the gills, leaving tail and head on; clean scales off and remove insides. Oil outside of fish thoroughly; lightly salt inside of fish and lay inside several large, dried dill sticks or a sprig of dill seeds and 2 slices of lemon. Salt and pepper fish on both sides; lay whole fish on its side on a large enough piece of heavy foil to wrap fish completely. Fold foil so that it is "hemmed" at both ends and along the length. We use our roasting pan and lightly grease the bottom, so that if any juices do escape and bake on, the foil will not stick to the pan and spill all of the juices.

Preheat oven to 350°. Cook the fish in its foil envelope for ½ to ¾ hour. Test for tender doneness. Do not overbake, since fish will fall apart and be hard to serve. To serve, lift meat off bones with a spatula or pie server, pouring natural juices over each serving.

INDIAN FISH SAUCE

Beat together ½ cup salad oil, ¼ cup each lemon juice, chopped parsley, and mint, ¼ teaspoon salt, ⅛ teaspoon cayenne pepper. Pour over broiled fish. When we have fresh dill leaves, we use these instead of mint.

FISH MARINADE

Soak prepared fish for about 2 hours in 1 part vinegar or lemon juice to 2 parts oil to cover. Add dill or chervil.

SORREL FISH SAUCE

Chop cleaned sorrel very fine and simmer in butter until all moisture in sorrel is evaporated. Pour sorrel butter over broiled fish.

Tips
Freezing fish: If you have a fisherman in the family or a chance to buy a quantity of fish at one time, here is how to keep them from drying out and losing their flavor in the freezer. Clean and prepare fish for cooking, then layer fish in a loaf pan as tightly as possible; pour cold water over them, being sure to cover the top fish. Freeze. When frozen solid, run warm water quickly over the pan to release the block of fish. Bag tightly and store in the freezer.

To test doneness of fish use a toothpick inserted in thickest part; lift slightly. If fish is no longer transparent, it is done.

When you have had fish for dinner, save all bones, leftover juices, and meat. Boil these with some onions for 1 hour; strain out bones and freeze to use as a fish chowder base in future.

A quick dip in boiling water will make fish easier to scale.

PEG'S BAKED STUFFED FISH

Select a fat fish 18 inches long from nose to tail. We like king mackerel or largemouth bass. Clean fish, scale, and remove fins. Leave head and tail on. Rub cavity with salt and lemon juice. Refrigerate while mixing stuffing. Preheat oven to 350º.

STUFFING
1 cup cooked shrimp or crab meat
3 tablespoons vegetable oil
3 stems celery, chopped fine
3 stems parsley, chopped fine
½ teaspoon salt

Dash of white pepper
1 clove garlic, minced or pressed
3 green onions, chopped
1 cup bread crumbs
1 cup water

Cut up the shrimp or crab meat fine, and sauté in vegetable oil. Cook it and all the other ingredients together until soft and of a consistency for stuffing. Oil fish thoroughly. Stuff fish and fasten closed using toothpicks. Slash fish short way 4 times. Follow wrapping directions for Baked Whole Fish (page 32). Cook at 350º, 10 minutes per pound.

OPTIONAL SAUCE TO POUR OVER FISH AT SERVING TIME.

⅛ pound butter, melted
⅛ teaspoon salt
  Dash pepper

½ teaspoon dill seeds
  Juice of 1 lemon

Place salt, pepper, and dill seeds in melted butter about ½ hour before serving time. When fish is on serving platter, mix lemon juice and butter and pour over fish.

SHRIMP AND AVOCADO MOLD

Make Lemon Gelatin Dessert (page 172), but use ¼ cup of sugar instead of honey.

3 tablespoons vinegar
5 drops of hot pepper sauce
¾ teaspoon salt
¼ teaspoon garlic salt
1 teaspoon crushed basil

2 tablespoons each chopped green
   onion, pimiento, green pepper
1 large avocado
2 hard-cooked eggs, sliced
1 cup cooked prepared shrimp

Add first 5 ingredients to the gelatin dessert. Chill until mixture mounds on spoon. Fold in onion, pimiento, and pepper. Cut avocado lengthwise into halves; remove pit and skin; slice. Fold into gelatin with eggs and shrimp. Place in 1½-quart ring mold. Chill until set. Serves 8 to 10.

ALICE MATTOON'S SHRIMP AND FISH CASSEROLE

½ cup milk
1 can shrimp or lobster bisque
3 drops hot pepper sauce
¼ teaspoon salt
   Dash of coarse pepper
   Slivered almonds

4 medium flounder filets, undersides
   preferred (or any other nonoily
   fish)
8 ounces frozen prepared shrimp or
   2 cups cooked fresh shrimp (save
   juices)

Mix, in bottom of greased casserole, milk, shrimp bisque and any juices from cooking shrimp, hot pepper sauce, salt, and dash of coarse black pepper. Put down a layer of ⅓ of the shrimp; lay 2 flounder filets, which have been cut crosswise in 2-inch strips, on top of shrimp; lay another layer of shrimp, then the balance of the pieces of flounder. Top with shrimp and sprinkle on top slivered almonds which have been lightly toasted in oven. Bake at 350° until bubbles show on top and casserole begins to brown. Serves 6 to 8 over ½ brown and ½ wild rice prepared according to package directions. If you buy the rice mixture in a package, do not use spices included.

MEAT SUBSTITUTES

"This present time of high prices for food-stuffs, should not pass without leaving us better qualified to cope with the return of the same conditions. If we learn our lesson well, we shall know how to take our old time supply of food and make it go 'farther'. For the truth is, women in general do not get the full value of the money expended for food. With too many of us the A.B.C. of economy is yet to be learned, and as we have said before in these pages, economy does not consist in going without, but in obtaining the greatest value possible out of what we buy, this means study on our part. And a little thought is what too many of us seem to be afraid of." (From The Boston Cooking School Magazine, June—July, 1910.)

BAKED BEANS

1½ cups dried beans
1 teaspoon salt

Small ham bone (optional)
¾ cup chopped onions

Cover beans with water and soak overnight. In morning, drain, cover beans with fresh water, bring to a boil, and simmer for 1 hour. We add, at this stage, the salt, small ham bone, if we have it, and ½ the onions called for. We believe this distributes the flavor and thus cuts down on baking time. Cool in water they have been cooked in. Drain, reserving cooking water, and add

Remaining half of onions
¼ pound diced salt pork
3 tablespoons dark molasses

¼ cup brown sugar
1½ teaspoons dry mustard
½ cup boiling bean water

Place in bean pot or casserole and bake, covered, in a slow oven (300º) for 3 hours. If they become dry, add a little reserved bean water. Uncover beans for last half hour of cooking time.

Tips
To keep your home-dried beans from getting wormy, add a bay leaf to container.

Baked beans are a heavy dish and benefit from the sharpness of orange rind or juice added as served. An ideal accompaniment for baked beans— fresh sliced tomatoes or crisp salad with clear French dressing.

LIMA BEAN CASSEROLE

4 cups cooked lima beans, or 1¾ cups dried beans, soaked over- night and cooked for 1½ hours
1½ teaspoons salt
½ teaspoon pepper

1½ teaspoons crumbled sage
4 small onions thinly sliced
1 cup grated Cheddar cheese
½ cup half-and-half
5 slices bacon

Turn half of cooked drained beans into the bottom of a greased 2-quart casserole. Mix together salt, pepper, and sage; sprinkle half the season- ings over limas. Arrange sliced onions over the layer of beans, then cover with remaining beans. Sprinkle the remaining seasonings, and top with grated cheese; pour half-and-half over all. Lay bacon slices across top of casserole. Bake in a moderate oven (350º) for 30 minutes or until hot and bubbly.

Tip

We buy Cheddar cheese a whole round at a time. This way it is less expensive per pound, and you have a handsome round wooden box when the cheese is gone. This can be sanded and painted for a child's sit-upon, mounted on legs for a sewing box, or as a transplant box for large plants—it can be set into the ground, will decay, and allow the roots to spread out.

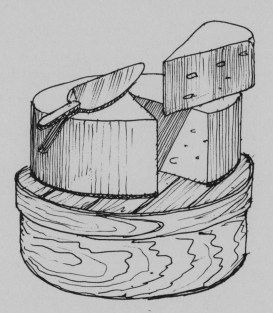

KATHRYN HALL'S CHEESE NOODLES

1 package fine noodles   1 pound mild Cheddar cheese

1 package fine noodles, salted and cooked until soft. Drain and place ½ of the noodles in buttered 9-inch by 13-inch pan. Cover with thick slices of unprocessed mild Cheddar cheese. Add remaining noodles and another layer of cheese. Put under a broiler until bubbles appear on top. This is a versatile dish and you could experiment with various types of cheeses and add an herb. Serves 6.

WELSH RAREBIT

1 cup milk
2 tablespoons cornstarch
¼ teaspoon mustard
½ teaspoon salt
2 tablespoons butter

1 egg
½ pound mild cheese
   Chopped fresh parsley or chopped hot
      peppers (optional)

Heat milk in double boiler to boiling point; add cornstarch (dissolved in a little cold milk), then mustard, salt, butter, egg, and cheese, grated. Cook a few minutes. Serve on toast or crackers. We often add chopped fresh parsley or chopped hot peppers for color or taste.

Tip
Any cheese dish will perk up in flavor and color contrast if you add finely chopped green onions.

CHEESE

Cheeses are foods of many textures, tastes, and odors. They can be used more than any other food element to augment and supplement others. Macaroni and cheese can be an ordinary dish. Here is an extraordinary way to prepare it.

TALL TREES MACARONI AND CHEESE

2 cups elbow macaroni
1 large onion, diced
1 teaspoon salt
1 cup grated mild Cheddar cheese
1 cup grated Swiss cheese

1 egg lightly beaten with ½ cup
   milk
½ cup diced sweet peppers
   Salt, freshly ground black pepper
¼ cup grated Parmesan cheese

Cook macaroni according to directions, except add 1 large onion and 1 teaspoon salt to the cooking water. Cook macaroni until almost tender.

Butter a 2-quart casserole; set oven at 350º. Mix drained macaroni, Cheddar and Swiss cheeses, egg and milk mixture, sweet peppers, and a good grinding of fresh black pepper, salt to taste. Place in casserole and sprinkle Parmesan cheese on top. Bake for about 30 minutes or until bubbles appear on top and mixture starts to brown.

PEG'S GREEN BEAN AND CHEESE CASSEROLE

¼ cup flour
2 cups milk
1 cup light cream
1 teaspoon salt
¼ teaspoon pepper
1 can mushroom soup, undiluted
2 teaspoons soy sauce
¾ pound Cheddar cheese, grated
1 medium onion, grated
1 pound fresh sliced mushrooms,
    sautéed and drained

3 packages frozen French-cut
    green beans (or about 4½ cups
    lightly steamed, fresh, French-
    cut beans)
1 5-ounce can water chestnuts
    or thin-cut prepared Jerusalem
    artichoke roots
1 small package slivered almonds

Mix flour, milk, and cream until smooth (see tip, page 68). Place this mixture in top of double boiler; add salt and pepper, undiluted mushroom soup, and soy sauce, and mix thoroughly. Cook, stirring frequently, until mixture thickens. Add grated cheese, grated onion, and mushrooms.

Remove from pan to a buttered casserole and lightly turn in green beans. Top with slivered almonds. Cook for 1 hour in 350° oven or until bubbly on top.

This party casserole can be made ahead and stored in refrigerator or freezer before baking. If in refrigerator, take out ½ hour before cooking. If frozen, allow 3 to 4 hours to thaw before baking. Serves 8.

CHEESE SOUFFLÉ

Prepare cream sauce (or use our White Sauce Mix, page 136).

Melt over low heat
3 tablespoons butter or margarine

Add and blend
3 tablespoons flour
¼ teaspoon salt
Dash of pepper

Slowly stir in
1 cup milk or vegetable stock

Cook, stirring constantly with wooden spoon until smooth and mixture comes to a boil. Reduce the heat and stir in
1 cup grated cheese

When cheese is melted, add
3 beaten egg yolks

Cook and stir these ingredients for 1 minute longer to permit yolks to thicken. Cool these ingredients. Whip until stiff
3 egg whites

Fold lightly into cheese mixture. Bake in an ungreased baking dish at 325° for about 40 minutes. Serve immediately.

Tip
Grate Cheddar cheese for any sauce, using coarse grater. Mixes better, melts faster.

A GOOD, EASY PIZZA

DOUGH

1 package dry yeast
1¼ cups warm water

3½ to 4 cups flour, sifted
½ teaspoon salt

Sprinkle yeast on warm water; stir to dissolve. Add 2½ cups flour and salt, stirring to mix well. Add another cup of flour and stir. Turn onto lightly floured board and knead until elastic. Place in greased bowl and let rise in a warm place until doubled. Turn out onto board and knead just enough to get out large air bubbles. Divide in half and roll into a circle. Stretch and fit into your pizza pans, which have been heavily oiled. This makes dough for 2 pizzas. If you do not have pizza pans, a jelly-roll pan may be used.

FILLING

1 8-ounce can pizza sauce
1 pound hamburger
2 large onions   } browned
1 clove garlic

1½ cups shredded mozzarella or
        Cheddar cheese
1 teaspoon oregano

Tips

If you are thinking of economizing by buying a quarter or half beef for the freezer, consider buying a whole round of beef instead. We find more well-flavored, lean meat in the round, fewer exotic things such as tripe and kidney (which my family won't eat). We ask for some steaks, some roasts, lots of hamburger and stew meat.

Ask for all the bones and fat; you've paid for them in your purchase anyway. The bones can be the base for many fine nourishing soups (see Braised Bones, page 142); the best suet can be kept frozen, or prepared ahead and frozen for Grandma Hunter's Turkey Dressing (page 58). Suet can also be hung on trees for the birds.

To cook frozen eye of round of beef rare, cook at 450° for 20 minutes. Take out of oven and cool. Just before serving, put back in oven at 450° for 25 minutes.

Rinse all empty ketchup, mustard, sauce, or relish bottles with a small amount of vinegar and water. Use to season stews, etc.

RICHER GRAVIES

Add 1 ½ cups of leftover coffee to 4 cups gravy. Browned flour adds flavor to gravy. Make by stirring flour in a dry skillet over very low heat. Watch and turn constantly—it can catch on fire. Browning reduces thickening power by ½, but it doesn't lump as plain flour does. Or add ½ square of bitter chocolate to the gravy.

Tip

Put some sugar in water used in basting meats. It adds flavor.

BOUQUET GARNI

These vary but usually include bay leaf, thyme, and parsley. Sometimes basil, sweet marjoram, summer savory, celery leaves, or any number of herbs are added. Take a square of about 4 inches of cheesecloth, put herbs in, and, picking up the four corners, tie with string. You can make these up ahead of time and have them ready for use in stews and soups, or give them to your friends. We use precut gauze sponges to make bouquet garni.

TALL TREES STROGANOFF

2 pounds bottom round steak
2 tablespoons butter
½ pound fresh mushrooms
1 small bunch green onions (tops and bottoms), chopped
1 medium-sized green pepper, chopped

1 cup beef stock or bouillon
Salt to taste
Dash of nutmeg
Chopped parsley
½ pint sour cream

Cut off all fat from steak; melt down fat in frying pan; discard remaining fiber. Cut steak into ½-inch cubes; brown in fat; drain. In butter, sauté mushrooms, green onions, and green pepper. Add beef stock to beef chunks and simmer until tender. Just before serving add sautéed vegetables and seasonings. Stir in sour cream. Serves 6.

VIRGINIA'S TALARINE

2 tablespoons vegetable oil
1 pound hamburger
1 large onion, chopped
1 green pepper, chopped
½ teaspoon salt
⅛ teaspoon Java cracked pepper
1 teaspoon oregano
1 8-ounce package fine egg noodles

1 can corn niblets or 1½ cups fresh corn
1 large can tomatoes or 4 large peeled fresh tomatoes
1 can pitted ripe olives
1 3-ounce jar Parmesan cheese
½ cup buttered bread crumbs

Put vegetable oil in skillet to heat; add hamburger broken into pieces, onions, green pepper, salt, pepper, and oregano, stirring constantly to keep from browning too much. In the meantime, cook noodles as per package directions, and drain. When hamburger combination is cooked, put noodles and mixture into large bowl and add corn niblets, tomatoes, and ripe olives.

In a casserole, put a layer of mixture, sprinkle with Parmesan cheese. Continue layering and adding cheese until it is all used up. Cover with buttered bread crumbs and bake in 375° oven for ½ hour. This can be made ahead and frozen or put in refrigerator for 24 hours. Serves 6.

MEAT LOAF

Place in a large bowl

2 pounds ground beef
1 egg
½ cup milk or vegetable stock
1 green pepper, chopped
2 medium-sized onions, chopped
½ cup chopped celery leaves

1 clove garlic, minced
1 cup soft bread crumbs
1 teaspoon oregano or basil
1 teaspoon salt
¼ teaspoon pepper

Mix well and place in a loaf pan. Bake at 350° for 1½ hours.

Tip
Bake meat loaf in an angel cake pan and cut oven time a third. The heat passing through the center tube bakes inside and outside simultaneously. The center can then be filled with sauce, or with mashed potatoes or other vegetables.

MEAT LOAF WELLINGTON

Prepare your meat loaf. Bake the loaf until nearly done. Let cool while preparing Flaky Pie Crust (page 180). Roll the pie crust until it is very thin and wrap it around the meat loaf, covering the loaf completely. Moisten the edges of the dough to hold them down. Bake the loaf in a quick oven until dough is nicely browned, about 15 minutes. Serve with leftover gravy or tomato sauce.

SPAGHETTI SAUCE

1 pound ground beef
1 tablespoon oil
2 medium-sized onions, chopped
1 green pepper, chopped
1 clove garlic, minced
½ cup celery, minced

1 teaspoon salt
2 teaspoons oregano or basil
¼ teaspoon black pepper
No. 3 can tomatoes or 4 cups fresh
    tomatoes, cooked

Sauté meat in oil and add all ingredients but tomatoes; cook until done. Add tomatoes. Simmer for about 1 hour until the sauce is thick.

Tip

You may take the leftover vegetables you have been saving in your freezer and add some vegetable stock (page 90); whirl in your blender until smooth. This is delicious added to your spaghetti sauce. Any leftover sauce and spaghetti can be put in a casserole, frozen, and used at some future time.

PARTY SPAGHETTI SAUCE

When you want a change from the usual spaghetti sauce, try this one.

½ cup olive or vegetable oil
2 cloves garlic
½ cup almonds
2 cups firmly packed fresh basil
    or 2 teaspoons dried, crumbled
    basil

1 teaspoon salt
¼ teaspoon black pepper
1 cup Parmesan cheese

Place oil and garlic in blender; cover and blend at high speed until smooth. With blades spinning, remove small cover; gradually add almonds. Blend until smooth. Add basil leaves a few at a time until well blended. Add salt and papper, then gradually add Parmesan cheese.

Cook 1 pound of spaghetti per label directions. Reserve ¾ cup cooking liquid, then drain off remainder. Put spaghetti with ¾ cup cooking liquid onto large platter, pour sauce over and toss until evenly blended. Serve with additional Parmesan cheese.

UNCOOKED TOMATO SAUCE

This is best made in the summer when you have tomatoes from your own garden.

5 medium-sized tomatoes, peeled and chopped
½ cup finely chopped fresh basil

Stir in
2 cloves garlic, minced
1 teaspoon salt
¼ teaspoon pepper

Pour over the above ingredients
½ cup olive or vegetable oil

Cover and allow to stand 1 hour at room temperature. Serve over spaghetti sprinkled with Parmesan cheese.

Tips

We buy a whole smoked or country ham. Have the butcher cut the protruding bone (which is full of marrow) into 3-inch lengths. The butcher also will cut two ½-inch slices from the center for you. This leaves you with two baking hams, two ham steaks, and pieces of bone with some fat and meat on them for making baked beans and lentil soup. Smoked ham should be frozen to keep.

Sometimes jelly has become too hard, or it failed to jell properly, or you have bits of several kinds left in jars. We use these to glaze our hams.

Baking bacon: We bake in quantity, 1 pound or 2 pounds at a time. Lay individual bacon strips, barely touching, to cover bottom of large broiler pan or several 9-inch by 13-inch cake pans. Bake (do not broil) at 350° for 15 to 20 minutes, or until desired crispness is almost reached. Remember, fatty foods continue cooking for a while after the heat is removed. Have ready two large, brown grocery bags, cut open to lie flat. Place bacon on paper to drain. Serve, or store in refrigerator or freezer to warm the next morning or to use crumbled on top of casseroles, spinach, etc. Do not forget you're baking bacon or you will have a fire. We prefer this method to top of the stove since we feel more of the harmful fat is removed this way, without splattering the stove or smoking up the kitchen. Because it cooks slowly, it is more tender. Because most bacon contains nitrites, we use it sparingly for garnishes. Country-cured bacon is generally prepared without nitrites.

In a large, black iron skillet, place sausage slices or links. Barely cover with water, and boil until water has disappeared and sausage is crisp. Turn as necessary.

ALL-OVEN COOKING FOR ECONOMY

An oven is an insulated box with the heating unit inside. It is an efficient way to cook if it is full, less efficient for fewer things cooked at one time. Most roasts, ham, chicken, meat loaf, etc., for which we use the oven, cook at temperatures from 325° to 375°. These temperatures make it quite practical to casserole-steam all other components of a dinner, while the meat is cooking.

Here are some menu suggestions:

Roast beef (more economical than steak), baked or oven-steamed potatoes (see page 84), oven-steamed green beans (do not allow to over-cook), oven-steamed ginger carrots.

Roast chicken, oven-steamed rice (see page 83), oven-steamed turnip greens, spinach, or collards.

Roast ham, oven-baked (in skins) whole yams, oven-steamed turnip greens, spinach, or collards.

Add a tossed green salad to any of those, bread pudding, steamed apples, or baked custard as dessert, and you will have some relaxed moments before dinner. Of course, any casserole dinner can be done the same way. Your whole-dinner oven cooking will only be limited by your imagination and study of the timing for various vegetables.

Tips

When salting the inside of a chicken or turkey, add some dried thyme and sage (crumbled fine) to the salt.

Use fresh carrot tops instead of parsley to decorate around a roast or chicken. Will look well, though not very edible except by rabbits.

We save chicken livers in the freezer until we have enough to make a party pâté or sandwich spread. Sauté livers in butter until brown, put in blender with butter they were cooked in and enough chicken stock to moisten. Add onion, salt, and pepper to taste. If you have cooked bacon or sausage, add this to livers for extra flavor. Proportion: 1 cup chicken livers to ¼ cup pork product.

YOUR CHICKEN STOCKPOT

When you have had chicken for dinner, save all bones from the plates for a soup or stockpot. Add the chicken carcass. Cover these bones with plenty of water, add sliced onion, bring to a boil, simmer for about an hour or until all remaining meat falls off the bones, strain, and use this broth as a base for soups, sauces, gravies. Boil bones again and you will have bastings for your next chicken; freeze and mark. Add some noodles to the broth for chicken noodle soup, and a crumbled leaf of sage and salt to taste. We do the same thing with any meat bones we have. Instead of sage, use sweet basil. These broths, cooled and with fat skimmed off, are the gourmet cook's basis for many fine dishes.

Tip
The addition of ½ teaspoon of vinegar to a 4-quart pot of boiling bones will draw more nutrients from the bones.

GRANDMA HUNTER'S TURKEY DRESSING

I can see her now, two nights before Thanksgiving, sitting before the fire in her living room filled with fine antiques, with a long wooden bowl in her lap and a long loaf of Clover Johnson's bread in one end of the bowl. She reached inside the crust and pulled out pieces of the bread. When this was completed and only a shell was left, she brought out the large piece of clear suet and tore off small pieces, discarding the fibrous part. We make two or three times this recipe at one time and package what is not needed for the turkey into plastic bags for stuffing roasting chickens. It is a drier dressing than most.

1 large loaf bread, crumbled—no crusts
1 pound clear beef suet; crumb it like bread; drench with flour

Place bread and flour-covered suet in large bowl; scatter nearly a box of poultry dressing and a tablespoon of salt. Add 1 box seeded raisins or currants and toss together with hands. Bake stuffing for 10 minutes in 350° oven. Cool, rub salt on inside of turkey, and stuff turkey.

PENNSYLVANIA CHICKEN POT PIE

1 stewing chicken, cut in pieces
4 cups water
1 teaspoon salt
¼ teaspoon dried sage
¼ teaspoon pepper
1 large onion, quartered
3 large potatoes
1 large onion

Drop the chicken pieces into boiling water with salt, sage, pepper, and quartered onion. Stew, covered, over a low flame for about 2 hours. Take chicken from the bones and put back into the broth; taste and correct the seasoning.

Cut potatoes into ¼-inch slices and lay them on top of the broth. Next, slice 1 large onion thinly and put it on top of the potatoes.

Make Best Dumplings Ever (page 23) and place on top of the onions. Cover with a tight lid and follow dumpling directions.

Serve in soup bowls accompanied by a chef's salad for a good hearty dinner. Do not forget to save the bones for broth.

Tips

Make good chicken soup from your chicken stock. To 8 cups of stock, add ½ cup uncooked rice or noodles and 1 teaspoon crumbled sage, salt and pepper to taste. Simmer until rice or noodles are done.

Marinate broiler chicken or baked chicken parts in a mixture of lemon juice and chopped onion the night before cooking. Drain and reserve marinade. Broil or bake chicken. Thicken marinade with 1 tablespoon of cornstarch mixed with water; heat until thick; add dash of salt and pepper and mint leaf cr two. Use as a sauce for chicken.

To control our animal fat intake, we often do not have gravy the first night we serve roast chicken, beef, or lamb, but refrigerate the juices overnight, skim off the fat, and use the essence with leftover chicken or meat. If you need to serve gravy right away, put it in a metal bowl or pan, set in a larger vessel of cold water and ice cubes. The fat will rise to the top and most of it can be skimmed off easily. Reheat for the table.

DAFFODIL EGGS

2 hard-cooked eggs, sliced (see page 131)
2 cups white sauce (see page 136)

½ teaspoon curry or mustard
Salt and pepper to taste

Mix and heat sauce in top of double boiler. Pour over sliced eggs on toast.

Tips

To fry eggs without fat, lightly grease a skillet which has a fitted cover using saved margarine papers. Break eggs into pan and cook covered, over very low heat, for about 5 minutes. Eggs will be tender, not tough.

Never use milk with an omelet; it toughens it. Use a tablespoon of cold water for a two-egg omelet.

EGGS AND SPINACH CASSEROLE

2 packages (12 ounces) frozen spinach, or 2 cups cooked fresh spinach
½ cup hot milk
3 tablespoons dry bread crumbs
⅓ cup soft butter
1 tablespoon grated onion
¾ teaspoon salt
⅛ teaspoon pepper
⅛ teaspoon nutmeg

1 cup white sauce (see page 136)
1 tablespoon lemon juice
1 teaspoon dry mustard
1 teaspoon grated onion
½ teaspoon salt
½ cup sautéed mushrooms
1 tablespoon minced parsley
4 hard-cooked eggs, sliced (see page 131)

Cook spinach. Drain. Add hot milk, bread crumbs, butter, 1 tablespoon grated onion, ¾ teaspoon salt, the pepper, and nutmeg. Mix well. Pack into buttered ring mold, and place mold in a pan of hot water. Bake in a moderate oven (350°) 15 to 20 minutes. Turn out onto a large, hot platter. Heat white sauce, lemon juice, mustard, 1 teaspoon grated onion, ½ teaspoon salt, mushrooms, parsley, and eggs. Fill center of ring with this mixture. Serves 6.

SUPER SCRAMBLED EGGS

4 eggs
3 tablespoons water
2 teaspoons butter

½ cup small cubes of Swiss cheese
½ cup diced onions or scallions
Salt and pepper to taste

Put eggs lightly beaten in top of double boiler. Add water and butter. Place over boiling water and stir gently until done. Add cubes of Swiss cheese and diced onions or scallions, salt and pepper to taste. Or add ½ cup leftover ham cut fine and 3 tablespoons dried browned onions, pinch of dry mustard. Or 1 cup chopped parsley and ½ cup diced green pepper.

POACHED EGGS

Gourmet cooks often prescribe a poached instead of a hard-cooked egg in a recipe since it is easier to judge doneness visually in poaching. To poach an egg, put your smallest frying pan, half full of water, on to heat. When bubbles form at edge of pan, put a drop or two of vinegar into the water. Stir a little well into the water and drop egg in immediately.

SOME SPICE IDEAS

Basil: Lamb, peas, cucumbers, egg salad, scrambled
                              eggs, tomato sauce, beef dishes

Bay leaves: meats, stews, sauces

Chervil: fish, egg dishes, soups, salads

Crushed hot peppers: add sparingly to spaghetti, ground beef mixture,
                              cheese dishes

Dill: beans, fish, in mayonnaise, with cucumbers,
                              salad pickles, cottage cheese, in rolls and
                              breads

Dry mustard: cheese and macaroni dishes, boiling cabbage,
mayonnaise, salad dressing, eggs

Fennel: use small amount—very strong herb—in shrimp,
poached fish, potato salad, meat loaf, and roast

Ginger: lamb, pot roast, carrots, sweet potatoes, cookies
and cakes

Marjoram: lamb and poultry, green beans or peas

Mint: lamb, tossed salads, fish, candies

Oregano: pizza, spaghetti sauce, scrambled eggs, green
beans

Rosemary: blends well with other spices, lamb, chicken,
shrimp, beans, cauliflower, turnips, oranges
and grapefruit

Saffron: chicken, yeast breads, rice

Sage: poultry, sausage, cream chowders, fish stuffing
and sauces, lima beans, eggplant, onions

Savory:	meat, chicken, scrambled eggs, omelets, cheese dishes
Thyme:	New England clam chowder, shrimp, dried beef, salad dressing
Turmeric:	creamed potatoes, macaroni, egg salad

OR, THE OTHER WAY AROUND, SOME COMPATIBLES

Beef:	bay leaves, sweet basil, garlic, oregano, sage, nutmeg, coriander, marjoram
Cabbage, brussels sprouts, broccoli:	caraway, dill, celery seeds, lemon balm
Carrots, squash, sweet potatoes:	nutmeg, ginger, ground cloves
Chicken:	dill, rosemary, sage, ginger, mustard

Fish: basil, savory, thyme, allspice, dill, fennel (use small amount—very strong), tarragon, mint, lemon balm

Green beans, limas, peas: mint, savory, thyme, dill, lemon, rosemary

Lamb: mint, cinnamon, curry, tarragon, rosemary, garlic

Onions: whole cloves, dill, ginger, rosemary

Peaches, pears, apples: anise, cloves, ginger, curry, nutmeg, lemon

Pork: cloves, fennel (use small amount—very strong), basil, caraway, sage

Stone fruits: almond flavoring, lemon balm

Veal: mace, oregano, paprika, basil, savory

STUFFED PEPPERS OR ZUCCHINI

6 peppers or 2 large zucchini
1 cup cooked rice
½ cup grated cheese or ½ pound
   hamburger

1 large onion, grated
A few celery leaves
Salt and pepper
Buttered bread crumbs

Wash peppers or zucchini. Cut tops from peppers, remove seeds, and reserve. Slice zucchini lengthwise. Remove and set aside the pulp, leaving about a ½-inch shell.

For The Peppers

Mix rice, cheese or hamburger, onion, celery leaves, top of peppers chopped, salt, and pepper. Fill the peppers and sprinkle with buttered crumbs; place in a 9-inch by 9-inch by 2-inch pan, with about ¼ inch water in the bottom of the pan. Bake in a 350° oven for about 45 minutes.

For Zucchini Squash

Cut up the pulp that you set aside into small, bite-size pieces, and in large bowl, mix with rice, cheese or hamburger, grated onion, celery leaves, salt, and pepper. Fill the shell and sprinkle with buttered bread crumbs. Place in a 9-inch by 9-inch by 2-inch pan, with about ¼ inch water in the bottom of the pan. Bake in a 350° oven for about 45 minutes.

Tip

These two dinners can be frozen before baking. Steam shells 4 minutes before filling them. Pack in plastic bags in one-meal-sized groups. We bake these right from the freezer for about 1 hour at 350º.

PEG'S CHICKEN BAKED IN RICE

1 teaspoon salt
½ teaspoon crumbled sage or 2
   leaves fresh sage, chopped
   Dash of pepper
2 cups chicken stock

1 cup uncooked rice
1 frying chicken, cut up
½ fresh green pepper,
   chopped (optional)
½ onion, chopped (optional)

Mix salt, sage, and pepper with chicken stock in bottom of a casserole. Add uncooked rice and, if used, green pepper and onion; stir. In the casserole, push down pieces of chicken into the mixture. Bake at 350º for 1 hour. Test chicken for doneness. If needed, cook ½ hour longer.

Tips

To mix dry ingredients such as flour, baking powder, or cornstarch with liquids of all kinds, measure liquid into clean jar; add dry ingredients. Screw cap tightly on jar and shake until smooth.

To test the heat of fat for deep frying, put in a piece of bread, and if it browns while you count to sixty, the fat is hot enough for raw foods. If it browns while you count to forty, it is right for frying precooked foods.

By "vin blanc" in meat sauces, the French do not mean white wine, because the wine turns to vinegar when it boils, "whereas if you use vinegar and sugar, they turn to wine in the cooking." This is from Queen Victoria's chef, Nicolas Soyer.

To grease a griddle, cut a potato in half, and when griddle is warm, run cut side of potato over the surface of the griddle. It works. To grease a casserole dish or baking pan, save butter or margarine wrappers in the refrigerator. Rub vessel to be greased thoroughly with one of these. There is always enough left on the wrappers to use this way.

ALICE MATTOON'S AMERICAN CHOP SUEY

Break up ½ pound hamburger into small pieces and fry until almost crisp. Drain; set aside. In same frying pan lightly sauté the following in 1 tablespoon salad oil:

½ cup chopped red and green
   sweet peppers
½ cup chopped onions

½ cup chopped celery stems
½ cup chopped zucchini or yellow
   summer squash

Stir while sautéing to avoid sticking. Remove from stove, add 1 cup cooked or 3 fresh tomatoes and cover. In saucepan, boil 1½ cups elbow macaroni and 1 teaspoon salt until just soft. Drain and add to mixture in frying pan. Add hamburger and ground pepper to taste; cover pan and set on low heat until macaroni is done. Serve with topping of crumbled bacon or chopped parsley.

STUFFED APPLES

Core apples, removing extra-large core. Stuff with partly cooked sausage or mincemeat. Bake slowly until apple is soft. Save cores for making apple jelly (see page 194).

STUFFED PEPPERS A LA TALL TREES

6 large green peppers
1 tablespoon vegetable oil
1 pound ground beef
2 medium onions, chopped
1 can hominy, drained
  Salt and pepper to taste

1 clove garlic, minced
¼ teaspoon basil
  Grated Parmesan cheese
1 can tomato soup
⅓ cup water

Wash peppers thoroughly; remove tops, seeds, and membranes. Chop tops. Heat oil in skillet; sauté meat, onion, and chopped pepper tops until brown. Stir in hominy, salt, pepper, garlic, and basil. Arrange peppers in baking dish; fill with mixture and sprinkle with grated Parmesan cheese. Pour soup, mixed with water over peppers. Cover; bake at 350° for 30 minutes; uncover and let brown for 10 minutes more.

PEPPER STEAK

2 pounds chuck roast
  Vegetable oil
2 cups water
2 bouillon cubes or your meat stock
2 sweet peppers, 1 green, 1 red, cut
  in strips

3 tablespoons cornstarch
2 tablespoons soy sauce
½ cup water
  Rice and soy sauce (optional)

Cut chuck roast (about 4 cups cut) in thin strips about 2 inches by 1 inch long. Brown meat in hot vegetable oil, then add water and bouillon cubes or meat stock; bring to a boil. Cover and simmer about 1 hour, or until meat is tender. Add sweet red and green peppers. Simmer 5 minutes longer. Blend cornstarch with soy sauce and water. Add this to meat mixture and cook, stirring slowly until thickened. Serve the pepper steak with fluffy cooked rice and additional soy sauce, if desired. Serves 4.

Tips

To marry or meld flavors, mix anything with multiple spices, herbs, or onions the day before.

If you are new to herb use, go slowly at first. Consult a good herb cookery book to learn which herbs are compatible with which foods. Nothing is more disastrous than the misuse of herbs in cooking.

STUFFED CABBAGE OR GRAPE LEAVES

Cook 3 minutes in rapidly boiling water 8 cabbage or 12 grape leaves (use the outer leaves of the cabbage). Remove from the water and drain well. Combine in bowl:

½ pound hamburger
1 medium onion, minced
1 clove garlic, minced
1 green pepper, chopped fine

A few celery leaves
1 cup cooked rice
¾ teaspoon salt
A few grains pepper

Divide the meat mixture into 8 parts, or 12 parts if using grape leaves. Put 1 part on each leaf. Roll leaves, tucking ends under, and secure with toothpicks. Place close together in a buttered baking dish. Dot each roll with butter. Pour into the baking dish ½ cup of stock or vegetable juice.

Bake at 375º until leaves are tender — about 45 minutes.

Tips

Stuffed cabbage and grape leaves freeze well. Freeze in plastic bags. When you remove from freezer, dot with butter and pour stock over them. Frozen portions will require 15 minutes more baking time.

If you wish to hide from the family the variety of vegetables you are using in a beef stew, put your vegetables and some vegetable stock in the blender to pulverize. Add this to the beef juices.

We also often thicken a stew with a leftover biscuit or two, rolls, or a bit of bread, pulverized in the blender.

We use leftover cooked liver by grinding it in the blender with enough beef stock to moisten, and a slice or two of cooked bacon, a sliced small onion, salt and pepper to taste. This can be used as a liverwurst substitute in sandwiches or for a party spread on crackers.

SAVE COOKING ENERGY

About fifteen years ago, we were strolling the lovely main street of Chatham, Massachusetts, after a day of sun and sea. In the window of a sporting goods store we saw a little stove contraption, for which claims were made such as "burns only newspaper," "cooks away the fats you should not eat." The stove had an unforgettable name, "Swaniebraai." We bought one and the next evening went to the beach with our stove, some hamburger, and some old copies of The Cape Cod Times. The wind was blowing wildly, but in spite of that we were able to light the newspaper in the stove. On went the hamburgers and in about 5 minutes we had the "char-broiled" hamburger that the fast-food chains advertise, but can't produce. We have never been without a Swaniebraai stove since that time. We never, rain or shine, broil meat or fish in any other way. Where that delicious smoky flavor comes from is still a mystery, but the fuel savings, recycling of newspapers, absence of kitchen smoky grease, and use of the fat drippings, which are so bad for us to eat, as the added fuel to the newspaper would be blessing enough alone. In addition, the very short fire-lighting and cooking time mean that the smoke produced is of short duration (less air pollution).

We use ours only out-of-doors and not in the fireplace as the manufacturer suggests may be done. Strangely enough our precious Swaniebraai cooks in pouring rain or falling snow (see Appendix, page 246, for source).

SWANIEBRAAI CHINESE FLANK STEAK

Flank steak, sized for guests
1 cup soy sauce, or more, if
    necessary to cover

1 large onion, sliced thin

Put steak and onion in a dish that can be covered; pour soy sauce over the steak. Marinate for 24 hours or more in the refrigerator; turn the steak once.

Take out of marinade and broil on Swaniebraai. Heat the marinade in a sauce pan to be spooned over the steak at the table.

TANGY SWANIEBRAAI STEAK

1 2-inch-thick steak sized for
    guests
Meat tenderizer
Olive oil

Prepared mustard (buy the best for
    this)
Freshly ground black pepper

Tenderize meat overnight. Slash fat edge of steak at 2-inch intervals. Brush both sides of steak liberally with olive oil; spread coating of mustard and sprinkle pepper freely. Place steak in a shallow dish in the refrigerator for 1 hour. Turn 2 or 3 times. For medium rare, broil about 12 to 15 minutes on each side.

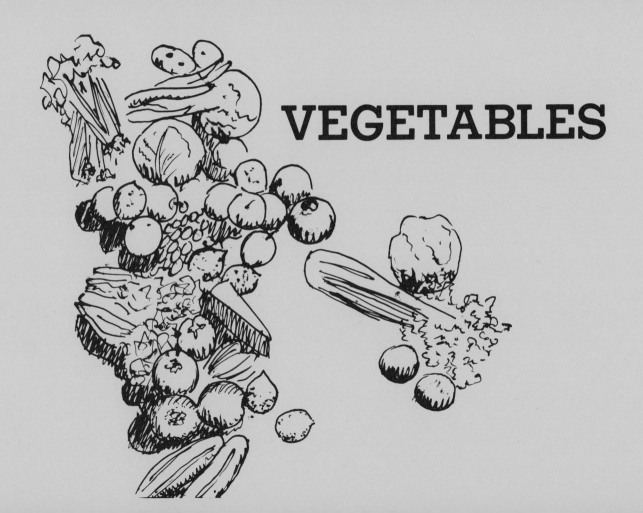

VEGETABLES

GREEN BEANS TARRAGON

2 packages frozen French-cut
   green beans
4 tablespoons butter or margarine
4 medium-sized green onions, including tops

2 tablespoons tarragon vinegar
½ teaspoon thyme
Salt and pepper
Slivered almonds

Cook the green beans in a small amount of boiling, salted water as directed on the package; remove from heat when they are just tender but not soft. Meanwhile, melt the butter or margarine in a frying pan. Finely chop the green onions and tops and sauté in butter until soft, about 5 minutes. Stir in the tarragon vinegar and thyme. Drain excess water from the green beans, and add to the onion mixture. Mix. Turn into serving dish and sprinkle top with nuts. Serves 6.

Tip

Farm labor and shipping of produce are expensive today, and many farmers are finding it increasingly convenient to allow customers to pick their own fruit and vegetables. The farmer usually charges less than wholesale prices for pick-your-own produce. Watch your local newspaper for ads for this privilege, because you and your family can give yourselves a pleasant outing, save dollars, and have garden-fresh vegetables and fruits this way.

NEW ZEALAND SPINACH

In praise of New Zealand "spinach." My father grew New Zealand spinach in our New Jersey and Massachusetts kitchen gardens. In fact, except for the commercially canned spinach which we had to eat in winter (I detested it because it was overcooked and tasted of the can), this is the only spinach we ate in our home. We loved it. New Zealand spinach is not a "true" spinach, but has all the healthful and flavorful characteristics, and more. We have always grown it and used it uncooked for salads, or cooked as a green, or for spinach soufflé. We freeze bushels for winter "green."

New Zealand spinach, which is a rambling, low plant loving hot weather, but surviving healthfully in cooler climes, has the cut-and-come-again characteristic appreciated by so many limited-season gardeners who are unable to manage multiple crops. When you gather New Zealand spinach for use, you pinch off the tender tip shoots down to leaves about 2 inches long. The plant, if grown in slightly alkaline soil, rich in natural nutrients, will send out four new shoots for the one you pick. When these develop, you will pick them too—and so forth. There is a special quality about these leaves, they look thick, healthy, and are especially enjoyable in a salad; they have the appearance of having caught tiny bubbles of dew.

A few years ago, Ted and I stood on Pebble Beach, California, watching the seals and brown pelicans, with a Bing Crosby Golf Tournament as background. I looked down for a moment, watched the seals for a while, then, a delayed reaction — we were standing in the midst of the most enormous area of New Zealand spinach I had ever seen. To be absolutely sure, I leaned down, picked and tasted a piece. It was my old friend from three thousand miles away. Since then I have planted New Zealand spinach in all hot, dry places as a summer ground cover. However, you must feed it well and see that it has at least a neutral soil to grow in. There is no other green leaf as adaptable as this.

Tip

In the fullness of summer, we like a table arrangement of fresh vegetables, purple eggplant, green zucchini, red tomatoes, red or green cabbage, a bunch of green onions—mix and match as you wish.

CABBAGE CASSEROLE

Small head green cabbage,
   about 1 pound
1 cup thinly sliced celery
1 cup vegetable juice
¼ teaspoon salt
1 can condensed, undiluted
   cream of celery soup or ½ cup
   cooked celery and 1 cup cream
   sauce

⅓ cup milk
4 tablespoons soy sauce
1 teaspoon minced onion
2 dashes hot pepper sauce
2 tablespoons butter or margarine
½ cup finely crushed crackers or
   homemade bread crumbs

Preheat oven to 350°. Shred cabbage coarsely to make 4 cups packed down. Place cabbage, celery, vegetable juice, and salt in a large saucepan; cover and boil 5 minutes; drain well. (Save vegetable water for soup.)

In a 1½-quart casserole, mix the soup, milk, soy sauce, onion, and hot pepper sauce; add drained cabbage and celery and mix well. In a small skillet, melt butter, mix in cracker crumbs. Sprinkle over cabbage mixture. Bake in oven until bubbly and topping is browned, about 40 minutes. Serves 4 to 6.

SPICED CABBAGE

1 medium-sized head of cabbage finely chopped
1 teaspoon whole, mixed pickling spices tied in small cheesecloth bag

¼ cup garlic-flavored vinegar
1 teaspoon salt
½ teaspoon fresh, ground pepper
3 tablespoons butter

Fill a pan with enough water to cover the cabbage, and add other ingredients except butter; bring to a boil and cook until just tender, about 5 minutes. Drain; remove bag of spices and add butter. Serves 8.

Tip

A little vinegar kept boiling on the stove while cabbage, cauliflower, or broccoli is cooking will prevent odor.

PEG'S OVEN-STEAMED RICE

Use margarine papers to grease inside of a 1-quart casserole (one that has a tight-fitting cover). Place 2 cups hot water and 1 cup rice in casserole; add ½ teaspoon salt; stir once; cover and place in oven. Cook in oven along with anything requiring about 350° for ½ to ¾ hour. Rice should be not quite tender, as it will continue to cook while the rest of the oven dinner finishes cooking. Remove from oven. Dot with butter and place on unlighted burner over oven vent to keep warm. We find that the ceramic-coated, heavy, cast-iron casseroles are best for oven steaming, since their lids fit very tightly and they hold heat well.

OVEN-STEAMED POTATOES

For a 1-quart casserole, 4 medium potatoes are about right. Slice about ¼ inch thick with skins on or off as you prefer. Stand as many potatoes on edge as possible; pour ½ cup lightly salted water over them. Cover them tightly and put in oven. Check for doneness after ½ hour. Serve mashed or "as is." Tiny new potatoes may be cooked this way also.

OVEN-STEAMED VEGETABLES

We also cook fresh or frozen vegetables this way. Keep quantity of water to ¼ cup and experiment with timing of different vegetables.

We do very little frying, but if you do and need to use the top of the stove for vegetables, try to find a store that carries these half pans. Together, they fit the large burner and in each you can cook a vegetable separately, thus saving the use of an extra burner. Think fuel saving!

CLEANING FRESH VEGETABLES

Chemicals cling to store-bought vegetables, and bugs and splashed dirt may be on your leafy garden vegetables. Here is a quick and thorough way to clean them. In a large bowl of lukewarm water, stir 2 tablespoons of salt (we use the cheapest salt we can find for this purpose); dip and slosh around your vegetables. Leave about ½ hour, then slosh again. Pour off this water and replace with cold water. Rinse thoroughly and store in refrigerator in damp paper towels or use immediately. Use recycled paper towels for counter cleanups.

Tip

Some vegetables produce for you twice. They have tops that are good to eat as well as roots that are important food. Some of them are:

Beets: greens for salads, roots and tops for vegetables

Celery: roots are excellent as main vegetable. Tops for
                      salads, soups, stews

Garlic: tops for flavorings, roots for flavorings

Onions: tops for flavorings and chopped in salads, roots for
                      vegetables

Radishes: greens for salads and to cook, roots for salads and to cook

Turnips: greens for salads and to cook, roots for vegetables

MARINATED FRESH VEGETABLES

If you have a vegetable garden, you will want to spend some time thinking of ways to utilize the bounty which pours from the garden all summer. Uncooked vegetables, fresh from the garden, have all of their vitamins intact and will provide you new taste sensations. Exciting hors d'oeuvres may be made by marinating the following for about 2 hours at room temperature, then refrigerating for an hour before use:

Baby zucchini and yellow summer squash: pick when about 3 inches long, cut long way into finger-sized sticks, leaving skins on.

Large, fresh lima beans, hulled. Celery stalks: 3-inch pieces. Baby green onions: cut green stem so that the small onion bulb and stem equal about 3 inches. Cauliflower heads: cut off blossom heads with a small piece of stem attached from main thick portion of the base of the head; if too large for a polite single bite, cut these into halves or quarters, including a portion of the flower head on each piece. Baby icicle radishes are superior in this marinade, cut in half the long way if too large. Green sweet peppers or ripe red sweet peppers sliced the long way. The sweet banana pepper, grown so much in the South, will add color either in its butter yellow, orange, or red stage. Asparagus tips ¼ inch thick and about 3 inches long. Jerusalem artichoke roots sliced into ¼-inch by 3-inch sticks. Very fresh eggplant, sliced into 2-inch sticks and peeled, can be used.

You can add to this list with other vegetables you have in your garden or find in the market.

THE MARINADE

8 tablespoons salad oil
2 tablespoons herb or wine
   vinegar
¼ teaspoon salt

¼ teaspoon dry mustard
Pepper to taste
Finely chopped onions or small
   garlic clove, chopped fine

To this add any herb which you like — about 1 teaspoonful, crumbled. Shake well in screw-top jar. Use either as salad dressing or marinade.

Tip

Save the thick base from which you have cut the flower heads of cauliflower and cut up into ¼-inch chunks for addition to a stew.

PEG'S GREEN GARDEN SALAD

New Zealand spinach tips, young radish tops, celery leaves and some stems; 1 big sprig of spearmint, small sprig of lemon balm, 10 wild onions, tops and bulbs chopped.

Mint and balm leaves should be removed from stem and torn by hand into small pieces. New Zealand spinach leaves should be plucked from pinched-off tips. This, instead of lettuce, is the base of your salad, so the volume of your salad is determined by the amount of spinach used.

Tips

In preparing greens for salads, never cut them but tear them into pieces. Cutting bruises the greens and makes them limp.

Add wafer-thin slices of an unpeeled bright red apple to a green salad.

Radish tops make a very excellent addition to any salad. Tear them fine. They also add dash and vitamins to cooked spinach.

VEGETABLE DELIGHT

½ cup olive oil
1 cup onions, chopped
½ cup green peppers, sliced
1 cup fresh lima beans

2 cups corn, sliced from cob
Water
½ cup parsley, chopped
2 cups zucchini, sliced
½ cup tomatoes

Brown onions and green peppers in oil. Add lima beans, corn, and a small amount of water. Simmer ½ hour. Add zucchini, tomatoes, and parsley. Cook over low heat for 45 minutes. Serve in bowls.

FOR VEGETABLE STOCK

Wash and save pea pods, parsley stems, tough asparagus ends, celery tops and strings, green bean ends, carrot skins, potato peels (if you wash them before peeling), less-than-salad-quality lettuce leaves. Cover with water and simmer for ½ hour; mash and strain. Freeze liquid for future use. Discard pulp.

Garlic has an incredible reputation for all sorts of fine healing and flavoring activities. If you are interested, you should consult some of the excellent herb books on the subject. We grow regular garlic and its more scarce cousin called elephant garlic, milder, but three times the size of the garlic in the stores. We know of only one place that has elephant garlic —Nichols Garden Nursery (see Appendix, page 246).

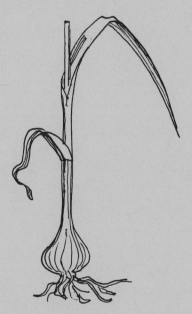

BAKED WHOLE ONIONS

6 medium-sized onions, skinned   2 tablespoons butter or margarine
   Juice of one lemon   Salt and pepper

Place onions in a greased casserole and pour lemon juice over them. Dot with butter, and salt and pepper lightly. Put on a tight lid. Bake at 325° for 1 hour.

Tips

When onions are low in cost, buy 50 to 100 pounds. Set aside a Saturday morning, and, remembering to save the cone and base (see page 93), peel and dice the onions. Fill pint-size bags and put in freezer.

If you have a way to dry onions, slice them into very thin chips, dry thoroughly, and store in airtight jars. To dry, place sliced onions on a window screen, cover with another window screen, and leave in the sun for 3 days. Bring in at night or if it is raining. If you are interested in dyeing fabrics, save your yellow outside onion skins and boil them for a saffron-yellow dye. You can also store this dye in sealed jars and use in cooking.

When stored too long, onions start sending out shoots. Cut the shoots off and chop fine for salads or soup toppings.

Tips

To get extra mileage from fresh onions, before peeling, carefully cut a circle around the root and up into the onion about ½ inch. Pull on root; you should have a small, cone-shaped piece with root attached. This may be planted, and within weeks you will have fresh onion tops for salad cr garnishes. In a few months, you will have fresh onions.

If you are plagued with wild onions in your lawn, or can find them in nearby unsprayed fields, use them by all means. (Do not use if you have put weed killer on your lawn.)
   Use the tops chopped fine instead of chives. Skin and cut off roots of the tiny onions; the skin will pull off easily when just gathered. Keep handy a pint jar of vinegar with ½ teaspoon of salt in it. Put these into the jar as you find them. These make excellent "cocktail onions". Refrigerate.

Tips

To keep avocados, artichokes, and other vegetables which turn dark when cut, place them in a bath of 3 tablespoons of vinegar to 1 quart of water. Fruits should be put in ¼ cup of lemon juice mixed with 1 quart of water.

To hasten ripening of tomatoes, place them in a plastic bag with 1 or 2 apples or a banana. Seal bag tightly.

To save space in your freezer, package soft things such as applesauce as flat as possible. We fill large plastic bags, flatten the food to about 1 inch thick, and freeze on a cookie sheet until stiff. Don't forget to squeeze out any air pockets.

VEGETABLE SOUP

1½ cups lentils, washed
7 or 8 cups water
4 beef bouillon cubes or your own stock substituted for water
1 medium-sized potato, peeled
2 bunches Swiss chard or beet greens
1 medium-sized onion, chopped fine

6 tablespoons salad oil
1 bunch fresh celery leaves
3 cloves garlic
¾ teaspoon salt
¼ teaspoon pepper
½ teaspoon cumin
3 tablespoons lemon juice
Fresh lemon slices

In a 5-quart kettle combine lentils with 7 cups of water and the bouillon cubes (or your own stock); cover and bring to simmer. Dice potato into about ½-inch pieces and add to simmering mixture. Wash and drain chard; cut off heaviest part of white stems; slice leaves in ½-inch-wide strips and add to the soup; simmer until lentils are tender, about 40 minutes. In a frying pan, sauté onion slowly in the oil, stirring often until soft and golden, about 15 to 20 minutes. Set aside about ¼ of the fresh celery leaves for garnish; finely mince remaining celery leaves and the garlic. Add celery leaves, garlic, and onions to soup during last few minutes. Stir in salt, pepper, cumin, lemon juice, and additional water if soup needs thinning. Serve with reserved celery leaves and lemon slices. Makes 10 cups.

BUTTERNUT SQUASH

Butternut squash is the most insect and disease resistant of the squash family, will produce bountifully in your garden. This handsome tan squash keeps well during winter and can be used in a variety of ways. Peeled, seeded, cubed and steamed, it makes a vitamin-rich potato substitute. Stuffed and baked, it is a hearty winter dish.

BAKED, STUFFED BUTTERNUT SQUASH

2 medium squash
2 cups shredded pineapple
4 tablespoons dark brown sugar

1 teaspoon salt
2 tablespoons butter

Cut each squash in half lengthwise. Do not peel squash. Remove seeds and pulp. (Save seeds for birds.) Scoop out inside of squash, leaving ½ inch all around. Chop squash "meat" fine. Mix with all other ingredients except butter. Fill cavity in squash and top with butter.

Bake in oblong pans for 1 hour at 350º, or until a fork inserted in the squash indicates tenderness.

ZUCCHINI SQUASH

Bush zucchini squash is one of the easiest vegetables for a beginner to grow. If you have any zucchini squash, you will have a lot of it. Of course, pick the baby ones to marinate, the ones 4 to 6 inches for slicing to steam, or for a casserole with onions and cheese. If you turn your back for a day and one of them grows a foot long, you can stuff it with the same stuffing as for peppers (see page 67). There is even a delicious soup you can make.

ZUCCHINI SOUP

3 pounds slender zucchini
¼ pound unsliced bacon
1 10 ½-ounce can consommé
3½ cups water
1½ teaspoons salt

¼ teaspoon white pepper
Garlic powder to taste
Sour cream
Chopped chives

Wash fresh zucchini squash—the slender ones are best for this—remove ends, and cut into chunks. Don't peel. Put these in a pot with unsliced bacon cut into 4 or 5 pieces (rind left on), consommé, water, salt, pepper, and garlic powder. Cook about 1 hour or until zucchini are completely tender. Remove bacon and press soup through a fine sieve or buzz in electric blender. This can be made a day or two in advance and reheated in a double boiler before serving. When you serve the soup cold, garnish with sour cream and chopped chives.

SQUASH "CURRY"

4 to 6 small yellow squash,
  unpeeled
1 medium onion, chopped
4 tablespoons butter
1 teaspoon turmeric or Oriental
  mustard
¾ teaspoon salt

½ teaspoon freshly ground or crushed
  black pepper
3 medium tomatoes, peeled and
  chopped
½ cup plain yogurt
1 teaspoon fresh tarragon or ¼ teaspoon, dried

Cut squash in cubes. Sauté onion in butter until starting to brown; add turmeric or mustard, and squash; stir and fry 3 minutes. Add salt, pepper, and tomatoes; cover; cook until tomatoes are mushy; add yogurt, turning heat as low as possible; cook a few minutes longer. Add no water. At last minute blend in tarragon. Serves 6.

Vegetables are at their very best nutritionally, and as to taste, when steamed until barely tender and still crisp. Vitamins are not lost in water and their flavor stays at its peak. Lightly salt after cooking. We use a triple-tiered Japanese steamer which is also important to us in blanching vegetables for freezing. These are usually available at Oriental food stores.

BAKED ACORN SQUASH

We often substitute baked acorn squash for potatoes. Cut squash in half lengthwise. Remove seeds and stringy matter. Salt lightly. Put 1 teaspoon butter or margarine and 1 tablespoon dark brown sugar into the cavity. Bake at 350° until a fork test shows squash to be soft. Squash that has been in storage for a few months benefits from 5 minutes of steaming prior to baking.

Tip

Nuts for you and the birds. When you prepare fresh squash or pumpkin, save the seeds. Rinse thoroughly in a strainer to remove as much fiber as possible. Then scatter on a newspaper to dry. When remaining fibers have become stiff, separate them from the seeds, rinse seeds once more, and dry. If seeds are plump and big, you can hull and roast them to eat in hand or use instead of nut toppings. If smaller, save them to mix with birdseed for winter food for your birds.

BOUNTIFUL HARVEST CASSEROLE

When your garden is pouring forth its riches, make this fine vegetable casserole.

Sauté in olive oil

2 large onions
2 large garlic cloves, chopped fine

Add

1 medium eggplant, cut into cubes
4 to 6 unpeeled medium zucchini,
    sliced thickly
2 large green sweet peppers, chopped

Stir and cook until soft. A little olive oil may need to be added. Then add

½ cup chopped parsley, stems and
    leaves
1 teaspoon dried basil or ½ cup
    fresh basil leaves, chopped
Salt and pepper to taste

Grease a casserole and stir the mixture into it. Add

4 large tomatoes cut into ⅛ sections

Cook in 300° oven until the tomatoes are soft.

Tips

To powder parsley, dip a bunch quickly into boiling water to make it a bright green. Put into a hot oven for a few minutes to dry thoroughly. Finish drying as it cools. Rub in fingers or through a sieve to break into fine flakes.

All the water that vegetables have been cooked in should be saved. For this purpose we keep a quart plastic container in the freezer and keep adding to it. Then we have vegetable juices to use in soups and in cream sauce in place of milk. We make our cheese soufflé using vegetable juices in place of milk. Many vitamins and minerals are left in vegetable cooking water. These nutritious juices add zest to many dishes—fewer calories than milk, too.

The small amount of vegetables that return to the kitchen in serving dishes are also frozen in quart plastic containers to be added to homemade soups.

We have become very fond of the small, white Tokyo Cross turnips. Ready for use in about 35 days, they are tender, gently flavored, and the tops are excellent for salad or greens. We pull them when they are about 3 inches in diameter. Here's one way to use them: Boil until medium soft; cut a flat area on the bottom, so they will sit on a plate without rolling over. Scoop out the inside (add removed portion to your greens), leaving a little cup. Cool. Fill the cups with lightly steamed fresh peas, cooled. Top with mayonnaise, and dill or parsley leaves as decoration. Chill until needed.

Tip

If you have too many cucumbers, peel, cut into chunks, steam, and freeze to add to vegetable soups or stews.

CUCUMBER SUMMER SOUP

3 cups peeled and diced cucumbers
2 cups buttermilk
½ pint sour cream

Salt and pepper to taste
Several sprigs of fresh dill leaves, finely chopped

Whirl cucumbers in blender. Add buttermilk; mix at slow speed. Remove from blender. Mix in sour cream, seasonings, and dill. If too thick, add more buttermilk to desired consistency. Serve ice cold. Serves 6.

MUSHROOMS

If you are not accustomed to thinking of mushrooms as a vegetable, consider them as such. Their dusky flavor is superior when they are raw. A dish fit for a king is lightly sautéed mushrooms on toast.

SAUTÉED MUSHROOMS

Clean mushrooms and slice lengthwise through cap and stem. On medium heat, melt ⅛ pound of butter, or enough to provide a good covering for the frying pan. Add mushrooms, sauté and turn until they shrink slightly and are a light brown; cover pan to steam for about 10 minutes. Salt to taste and serve over toast.

MUSHROOM DIP

¼ cup milk or buttermilk
8 ounces cream cheese
1 tablespoon minced onion

1 cup finely chopped mushrooms
½ teaspoon salt
Minced parsley

Beat milk, cream cheese, and onion until mix is light and fluffy. Sauté the mushrooms lightly and drain them thoroughly. Fold mushrooms and salt into the mix and top with finely minced parsley. Use as a dip with crackers or as a spread on small pieces of your homemade bread.

Raw mushrooms are superb added to a salad. Their fragrance is of the secret deeps of the earth.

VIRGINIA'S BLENDER TOMATO ASPIC

Place in blender

2 pounds ripe tomatoes, peeled, cut in chunks
1 medium onion, peeled, cut in chunks

1 bay leaf, crumbled
1 teaspoon dried dill
1½ teaspoons salt
½ clove garlic

Whiz until pureed, about 10 seconds. You may have to do this in two batches.

2 tablespoons unflavored gelatin
⅓ cup water
2 tablespoons vinegar or lemon

1 tablespoon sugar
Salad greens

Sprinkle unflavored gelatin over cold water and vinegar or lemon juice in a metal cup and set in a pan of hot water over low heat to melt. Stir into the puree. Add sugar. Pour into 1-quart mold. Chill until firm. Unmold and garnish with salad greens. Serve with Virginia's Cucumber Dressing (page 132).

TOMATO ASPIC (An Old Recipe)

To a pint of rich and highly flavored beef, chicken, or veal broth, add 1 cup cooked tomatoes, with salt and pepper as needed. Also add 2 packages of gelatin softened in ⅓ cup of cold water, and crushed shells and slightly beaten whites of 2 eggs. Stir constantly over the fire until boiling; let boil three minutes, then draw to a cooler place to settle. Skim and strain through cheesecloth wrung out of boiling water, turn into molds, and let chill.

EGGS BAKED IN TOMATOES

Select round, medium-sized tomatoes; cut a thin slice from the top of each and scoop out enough of the pulp to leave a space large enough for an egg. Season the cavities with salt and pepper and drop an egg into each. Cover the bottom of the baking pan with hot water or butter, put the tomatoes in and bake about 12 minutes at 350º. Season with butter and serve on toast; garnish with parsley.

STUFFED TOMATOES

Mix grated Cheddar cheese with some of the tomato pulp scooped out, and add chips of bacon. Top with bacon chips and a sprinkle of cheese. Broil.

CALIFORNIA TOMALIMA

1 medium onion, coarsely chopped	4 slices cooked bacon
1 cup cooked and mashed tomatoes	2 cups lima beans
Pinch of dried or fresh rosemary leaves	Tomato juice
	Salt and pepper

Sauté onions in butter. Stir in mashed tomatoes, rosemary, and bacon. Cook for 10 minutes. Add lima beans and continue to cook until beans are tender. You may need to add some tomato juice to prevent mixture from sticking before beans are done. Salt and pepper to taste.

CUCUMBER ASPIC

2 cups peeled, seeded, diced
    cucumbers (3 to 4 medium)
Salt
½ teaspoon sugar
3 envelopes unflavored gelatin
1 cup cold water
¼ cup vinegar
1 teaspoon salt
2 tablespoons chopped fresh mint
    leaves

2 slices onion, chopped
⅓ cup parsley, leaves stripped off
    stems
1½ cups sour cream
¼ cup mayonnaise
¼ teaspoon hot pepper sauce
Fluted cucumber slices
Fresh dill or mint sprigs

Sprinkle cucumbers lightly with salt and sugar; let stand 20 minutes. In saucepan, sprinkle gelatin over cold water and vinegar. Stir over low heat until gelatin is dissolved. Add 1 teaspoon salt and mint leaves. Drain cucumbers; place in blender with onion and parsley. Whiz until pureed. Pour in liquid gelatin and blend a few seconds until smooth and tiny green flecks of parsley and mint are still evident. Refrigerate, or quick-chill in freezer about 30 minutes until thick and heavy, but not set. Beat in sour cream and mayonnaise. Season with hot pepper sauce and a little more salt if needed. Pour into 1-quart mold; cover and chill until set, 3 to 4 hours. Unmold; garnish with sliced cucumbers and bouquets of dill or mint.

GINGER CARROTS

4 cups carrots, sliced about ¼ inch
   thick
1 tablespoon oil
1 clove garlic, minced
2 teaspoons fresh ginger root,
   chopped fine

1 teaspoon water
1 teaspoon salt
1 teaspoon sugar
Chopped parsley
Sesame seeds

Cook carrots about 5 minutes, drain and cool. Heat frying pan with 1 tablespoon oil; stir in garlic and ginger root. Stir quickly until they start to brown, about 30 seconds. Add carrots, water, salt, and sugar. Keep turning with spatula until heated through (about 2 minutes). Turn into warm serving dish; garnish with chopped parsley and sesame seeds.

TALL TREES SWEET POTATOES

2 pounds of sweet potatoes
¼ cup milk
1 egg
½ teaspoon cinnamon
½ teaspoon nutmeg

4 tablespoons melted butter
Salt and pepper to taste
2 grapefruit
⅓ cup dark brown sugar

Peel and cut up sweet potatoes in thin slices. Cook until soft in boiling water. Drain and mash until smooth. Beat potatoes, milk, egg, cinnamon, nutmeg, and ½ of the butter; season to taste. Place mixture in casserole.

Cut skin and white membrane from grapefruit. Tear sections apart gently and lay on top of potatoes. Top with remaining butter and brown sugar. Bake in open casserole at 350° about 35 minutes or until topping is browned.

Tips

Fast potatoes: Boil in jackets after slicing across ¼ inch thick. Partially mash with salt, pepper, and butter.

If you must peel potatoes (in all cases possible, leave skins on since they are full of vitamins), you will want to keep your fingers unstained. To do this, peel potatoes before washing; wash them thoroughly after peeling. Grandmother King taught me this.

For dry boiled potatoes, when nearly done, drain off all water; dry potatoes with clean cloth. Put back on stove over low heat for a few minutes with lid removed.

Late in the season when potatoes sometimes shrivel, put a handful of salt in a paper bag with the potatoes. In a week or so they will fill out again and cook better. (From handwritten cookbook of early 1900's.)

SOME OLD WAYS OF KEEPING VEGETABLES AND APPLES

Potatoes should be put into the cellar as soon as they are dug. Lying exposed to the sun turns them green and makes them watery. Some housekeepers place sod over the barrels of potatoes not in immediate use. To prevent them from sprouting in the spring, turn them out upon the cellar floor. Do not use potatoes with any green on them.

To thaw frozen potatoes, put them in hot water. To thaw frozen apples, put them in cold water. Neither will keep long after being frozen.

Cabbage should be buried in sand, with the roots upward. Celery should also be buried in sand. Turnips and beets should be put in a dry part of the cellar. Carrots keep anywhere. Onions keep best spread, and in a cool place, but do not freeze. Parsnips are best buried in a pit in the garden and not opened until March or April in cold parts of the country. Squash should be kept in a dry place and as cold as may be without freezing.

Apples should remain out-of-doors in barrels until weather becomes too cold. Moisture will accumulate on them; they should be picked over several times during the winter, as one defective apple injures all its neighbors. If they are moist, wipe them.

Tips

Cook a few pea pods with peas to heighten flavor.

Add a few thin slices water chestnuts or Jerusalem artichoke roots to green beans.

Leftover peas and rice can be combined for a salad with clear French dressing.

If you grow your own potatoes, you can always slip your hand under the mulch and steal a few tiny potatoes. Steam these with fresh or frozen peas. Add crumbled bacon and serve.

Cook lettuce leaves with fresh peas. Remove leaves after cooking if any are left.

GREEN TOMATOES

When the first frost comes, there are always green tomatoes on the vine. Some people pull the whole vine, hang it in a dark, cool place, and use the tomatoes as they ripen. They will also ripen if wrapped in newspaper, but will need frequent sorting. We have so much produce to store in bulk in the fall, that we try to use green tomatoes as soon as possible. Here are two ways:

GREEN TOMATO SAUCE

8 green tomatoes
¼ cup flour
¼ cup butter or margarine
2 teaspoons salt

Dash of pepper
1 tablespoon sugar
½ teaspoon steak sauce
½ cup light cream

Chop up the tomatoes and toss them in flour. Melt butter or margarine in a large skillet, put in tomatoes, and cook, stirring frequently, until tomatoes are soft. Season with salt, pepper, sugar, and steak sauce. Cover and cook about 5 minutes. Pour in the cream and cook slowly until sauce is heated through. Delicious served over hot biscuits or toast. Serves 4 to 6.

STUFFED GREEN TOMATOES

1 egg
½ cup shredded Swiss cheese
1 slice white bread, crumbled
½ teaspoon salt

Dash pepper
Pinch of dried basil
3 large green tomatoes
Paprika

Start your oven at 375° or moderate and get out a shallow baking pan. Beat the egg with a folk slightly; stir in cheese, bread, salt, pepper, and basil.

Slice each tomato in half, crosswise, and scoop out the center with a teaspoon. Chop scooped-out tomato fine, and stir into egg-cheese mixture.

Place tomato shells in baking pan and fill the centers with cheese filling. Sprinkle paprika on top and bake 40 minutes. Serves 4.

Tips

Summer squash is such a bland vegetable that it needs all the help it can get. Add any or all of these to top of cooked squash: crumbled bacon bits, dried onion bits browned in the oven, or mashed, hard-cooked egg.

To roast corn on the cob, pull back husks from corn and remove silk (use a vegetable brush gently). Fold husks back to cover cob and tie at open end. Soak corn in salted water for 5 minutes, then drain. Roast on grill for 10 minutes (hot fire). Turn often. We make our "ties" by stripping a few husks and ripping them lengthwise.

STUFFED EGGPLANT

Cut eggplant in half; steam or boil for 12 minutes. Remove most of pulp from shell; mix equal amounts of diced raw tomatoes, green peppers, and onions; mix in eggplant pulp, salt, pepper, basil, and oregano. Bake in oven 20 minutes.

Tip

When we have sweet peppers in the garden, we chop them or cut them in strips to store in small bags in the freezer to add flavor and color to winter casseroles. Steam 3 minutes and cool before freezing.

SALADS

Tips

Nasturtium leaves are high in vitamins. In making any green salad, use them liberally. Just before the first frost, gather all leaves, clean, and cut them gently. Steam 2 minutes and keep in freezer for adding to delicate soups, or freeze fresh, unsteamed, and whole, to break into tired winter salads.

Tender beet greens are a color and taste treat used in green salads.

Before putting lettuce to crisp in refrigerator, sprinkle the leaves with a few drops of lemon juice, to prevent discoloration.

When working with a number of herbs and onions or garlic, mix them with a small amount of water or vinegar, depending on the recipe, the day before. Do not refrigerate. This allows the flavors to "marry."

SPINACH SALAD

You can prepare the salad and dressing ahead; mix them together just before serving.

1½ pounds spinach
8 ounces fresh bean sprouts
½ pound raw mushrooms, sliced
1 can (5 or 6 ounces) water
    chestnuts, drained and sliced,
    or Jerusalem artichokes,
    peeled and sliced

5 slices bacon
⅔ cup salad oil
⅓ cup red wine vinegar
⅓ cup finely chopped onions
2 tablespoons steak sauce
    Salt and pepper
2 hard-cooked eggs

Trim and discard the tough spinach stems; rinse the leaves well, pat dry, and break into bite-sized pieces. In a large salad bowl, combine the spinach, bean sprouts, mushrooms, and water chestnuts. In a frying pan over medium heat, fry bacon until crisp; drain and crumble into the spinach. Cover and refrigerate.

In a small bowl or jar combine the oil, vinegar, onions, and steak sauce; shake or stir to blend. Cover and chill.

Just before serving, pour dressing over spinach and toss gently until well mixed; season to taste with salt and pepper and garnish with the sliced eggs. Makes about 8 servings.

CUCUMBERS IN SOUR CREAM

12 cucumbers
6 hard-cooked eggs
  Lettuce, torn in bite-size pieces
1 cup sour cream
½ teaspoon vinegar

Mustard
Sugar
Salt
Pepper

Clean, peel, and slice cucumbers. Slice eggs lengthwise in 4 pieces, removing yolks. Place cucumbers, sliced egg whites, and lettuce in a bowl. Make a dressing by rubbing egg yolks through a sieve and adding sour cream, vinegar, mustard, sugar, salt, and pepper to taste. Pour over cucumbers.

FRESH PEA SALAD

2 cups peas
20 paper-thin slices Jerusalem ar-
    tichoke root or water chest-
    nuts
½ cup thinly sliced celery stems
½ cup grated carrot
¼ cup finely chopped green
    onions

1 mild white onion, sliced thin
  Sylvia Shopen's Dressing (page
   133)
Lettuce or New Zealand spinach

Newly picked, raw, fresh baby peas are a superb base for this summer salad (for winter you could use frozen peas thawed quickly by running hot water over them). To peas in a bowl add slices of Jerusalem artichoke root or water chestnuts, celery stems, carrot, green onions, and onion. Over this pour marinade of Sylvia Shopen's Dressing. Chill for about 1 hour; drain off marinade. Serve on a bed of lettuce or New Zealand spinach. Reuse marinade in spaghetti sauce (see page 52).

PARTY POTATO SALAD

12 medium-sized potatoes, washed and cooked in their skins
½ cup chopped parsley
¼ cup chopped green pepper
¼ cup chopped green onions, tops and bottoms
¼ cup chopped nasturtium, radish, or watercress leaves
¼ cup chopped celery tops

1 cup mayonnaise (page 129 or 130)
¼ cup clear French dressing (page 134)
1½ teaspoons salt
½ teaspoon pepper
1 teaspoon dry mustard
Paprika, pepper jelly (page 192), or pimiento (page 206)

Peel and thoroughly cool potatoes. Dice. Mix ¼ cup of chopped parsley with the next 4 ingredients; take out about ½ cup of the greens and add to rest of parsley; set aside. Toss remainder of chopped greens with potatoes. Combine mayonnaise, French dressing, and seasonings. Taste and add more salt if needed. Add to salad and toss to mix well. Pack in 8-inch by 8-inch by 2-inch pan or shallow dish. Sprinkle reserved parsley mixture over top. Chill. Lift out servings with a pancake turner. Sprinkle on top, paprika, tiny cubes of pepper jelly, or pimiento.

Tip

When boiling potatoes for a salad, we add salt, an onion, some parsley, one garlic clove, and several celery tops. These flavors penetrate the potatoes.

TOMATO JELLY RIBBON LOAF

We use an interesting mold for a special company dish. We find the nonstick sprays a great help in unmolding a complicated shape. Our collection of antique molds gives us a lion, a lamb, a rabbit, a bird on its nest, and many other shapes to use for special occasions.

THE TOMATO JELLY

Mix

¼ cup cold water

2 envelopes unflavored gelatin

Puree in blender

3 cups fresh, frozen, or canned
  tomatoes
4 sprigs parsley, chopped
1 stalk celery, chopped
2 tablespoons diced onions

Dash of hot pepper sauce
1 tablespoon lemon juice
½ teaspoon sugar
½ teaspoon basil

Place blender mixture in a large saucepan. Bring just to boiling. Remove from heat and stir in softened gelatin. Mix thoroughly. Set aside to cool.

THE RIBBON

¼ cup mayonnaise (homemade preferably, see page 129 or 130)

1 large package cream cheese
½ cup chopped chives or wild onion tops

Mix with beater until smooth.

Spray your mold with nonstick spray; pour ½ tomato mixture into mold. Put in freezer compartment for ½ hour, then move to refrigerator until stiff. Keep the second half of this mixture in a warm place. When first layer of tomato is stiff, spoon on the cream cheese mixture, then the remainder of the tomato. Set in refrigerator until stiff. Unmold on lettuce leaves.

HOT POTATO SALAD

6 slices bacon
½ cup cider vinegar
2 medium onions, thinly sliced
3 potatoes, peeled and thinly sliced

Salt
White pepper
Paprika

Dice and cook bacon until crisp. Remove and keep warm. Pour vinegar into the bacon fat after it has cooled. Add onions and cook until tender.

Add potatoes to onions, salt and pepper to taste. Cover and cook on low heat for 10 minutes. Just before serving sprinkle with paprika and add diced bacon, stirring them in quickly.

WATERCRESS SALAD

Wash the cress well; dry in a clean towel. Chop an onion, 2 radishes, 1 teaspoon grated horseradish. Serve on hearts of lettuce leaves with mayonnaise.

CARROTS, MUSHROOMS, AND ASPARAGUS

Place thin strips of cooked carrots and lightly sautéed mushrooms with cooked asparagus tips in a flat dish. Cover with French dressing. Chill. When ready to serve, arrange on a bed of lettuce.

SALAD DRESSINGS, SAUCES, MARINADES

WITH THE AROMATIC HERB, BY MRS. E. M. LUCAS

"It is the fashion of the day to cultivate the antique, from our grand-mother's gowns to the decoration of her house and even her garden. So the old-time fancy for the sweet, aromatic herbs is being revived more and more every year, and the borders of our gardens are made fragrant by the sweet wave of incense from the mingling of thyme, tansy, sage and mint—an odor inexpressibly richer than any myrrh. Not only have these sweet smelling things been cultivated by the people of the present century, but many of them were in common use among the ancients; they have been praised by poets, studied by philosophers, reverenced by the ignorant, and prized by the physicians for ages." (From The Boston Cooking School Magazine, February and March 1899.)

MARGARET KING'S MAYONNAISE

I took the first step toward cooking when I learned to hold and pour out the bottle of oil while my mother hand-beat her mayonnaise. Here is her recipe:

Break 1 large egg into a bowl. Beat until frothy; add a few drops of salad oil; beat again. Continue this process until mixture starts to thicken, then add oil faster, beating thoroughly each time until very stiff. Beat in 1 tablespoon cider vinegar, then add 1 teaspoon salt, ½ teaspoon black pepper, 1 teaspoon mustard, and the juice of 1 small garlic clove or ⅛ teaspoon minced garlic. The oil must be added slowly at first in order that oil and egg do not separate later in the making.

VIRGINIA'S BLENDER MAYONNAISE

1 egg
2 tablespoons vinegar
½ teaspoon salt
⅛ teaspoon pepper

1 clove garlic
½ teaspoon dry mustard
1 cup vegetable oil

Put everything but oil in blender. Add to mixture ¼ of the oil and whirl for a few seconds. Take off the small lid of blender and pour in the rest of the oil slowly. Turn blender off immediately. Stir mayonnaise and put in glass jar. Refrigerate. We thin this by hand, stirring in a little milk. Makes 1½ cups.

MARGARET KING'S HARD-COOKED EGG DRESSING

2 hard-cooked eggs
2 tablespoons mayonnaise
½ cup oil
¼ cup vinegar

½ teaspoon sugar
½ teaspoon salt
Black pepper
Pinch of dry mustard

Mash eggs; mix with mayonnaise; add oil, vinegar, sugar, salt, pepper, and mustard. This is the crowning glory of a spinach salad or to use with Chinese cabbage, on tomatoes, as well as on a lettuce salad.

Tip

To hard-cook eggs, always start eggs in cold water and bring to a boil slowly. Turn off heat and cook 5 minutes. This method will prevent cracked shells and rubbery whites. Virginia had a small implement which punches a hole in the end of the egg, preventing broken shells.

CHRIS HUNTER'S SALAD DRESSINGS FOR A BIG PARTY

BLUE CHEESE DRESSING

4 cups mayonnaise
½ cup buttermilk

¼ pound blue cheese

Put ingredients into a large bowl and use electric beater at medium speed until the desired consistency is reached.

THOUSAND ISLAND DRESSING
4 cups mayonnaise
2 cups undiluted tomato soup

1 cup sweet relish
2 tablespoons vinegar

Put ingredients into a large bowl and use electric beater at medium speed until the desired consistency is reached.

VIRGINIA'S CUCUMBER DRESSING

Stir into 1 cup sour cream, salt and ground pepper to taste.
Just before serving, blend in one peeled, finely chopped, and drained cucumber.

JIM BRUNER'S ROQUEFORT DRESSING

1 cup mayonnaise
1 cup sour cream

1 3-ounce piece Roquefort cheese

Put all ingredients in blender; whirl until mixed; put in jar and re-frigerate. This dressing will keep about 10 days.

SYLVIA SHOPEN'S DRESSING

Sylvia always had a way with salads. After her guests arrived, she would prepare the salad, her hands gently and deftly breaking up the greens to make it. This is her French dressing:

6 tablespoons cider vinegar
2 good pinches of dried tarragon
1 teaspoon salt
¾ teaspoon white pepper
½ cup sugar
¾ teaspoon dry mustard

¾ teaspoon paprika
1½ teaspoons mustard seed
2 teaspoons celery seed
½ teaspoon curry powder
12 tablespoons salad oil

Heat cider vinegar and steep the dried tarragon in it. Mix together salt, white pepper, sugar, dry mustard, paprika, mustard seed, celery seed, and curry powder. Add the hot vinegar, tarragon and all, to the dry ingredients. Add salad oil and mix vigorously. Chill; mix again just before using.

This dressing will keep for many weeks in the refrigerator. The flavors will meld during this time and the dressing will be even better than when newly made.

Tip

Whenever the quality of the food will not be adversely affected (as it is in making breads—see page 16), make double or triple a recipe and refrigerate or freeze the extra portions. This not only saves personal energy, but fuel energy and time spent on cleaning up.

CLEAR FRENCH DRESSING AND MARINADE

¾ teaspoon salt
1 clove garlic, crushed
  Pinch dry mustard

3 or 4 tablespoons vinegar
¾ cup salad oil
  Generous grinding black pepper

With a whisk, beat salt, garlic, and mustard into the vinegar; then beat in oil in small portions until sauce is smooth and lightly thickened. Season with pepper.

Tip

Clear French Dressing can be used in many ways—as a marinade for meats, to brush on hamburgers or spareribs.

PEG'S MARINADE

Use with fresh vegetables or to soak meat for 2 hours.

To 1 cup tarragon vinegar add cloves, bay leaf, chopped garlic clove, chopped onion, chopped parsley, and fresh dill.

A saying in a Pennsylvania Dutch family by a mother to her daughters: "Kissin' wears out, cookin' don't!"

WHITE SAUCE MIX TO STORE FOR QUICK USE

Into a bowl, measure 2 cups nonfat dry milk, 1 cup enriched flour, and 1 cup or ½ pound margarine. Cut in margarine until the mixture is like fine crumbs. Mix is made! Store in covered container in refrigerator up to 4 months.

To make 1 cup medium white sauce, measure ½ cup of mix into pan; add 1 cup cold milk or water; season with salt and pepper; stir well. Cook over low heat, stirring constantly until thick. For extra flavor use tomato sauce, chicken or beef stock instead of milk or water.

WARTIME HOLLANDAISE

1 cup medium white sauce (hot)
2 tablespoons mayonnaise (see page 129 or 130)
1 tablespoon lemon juice

Mix ingredients in top of double boiler, stirring. Do not allow to get too hot—it will curdle.

HOLLANDAISE SAUCE

Beat ½ cup butter to a cream, then beat in, one at a time, the yolks of 4 eggs, with a dash of salt and pepper. Add ½ cup boiling water and 2 tablespoons lemon juice and cook over hot water, stirring constantly until mixture thickens.

TWO SAUCES FOR HAM

ONE

1 jar currant jelly or other sharp   3 tablespoons prepared mustard
  jelly

Stir over hot water in a double boiler until melted and hot.

TWO

½ cup mayonnaise   2 tablespoons prepared mustard
2 tablespoons horseradish

You can keep this in the refrigerator ready for use.

BOOTS BRUNER'S SWEET AND SOUR SAUCE

¼ cup vinegar
½ cup water
  Pepper, just a dash
1½ teaspoons soy sauce

5 tablespoons brown sugar
  Catsup, to taste
1 clove garlic, chopped
  Dash of hot pepper sauce

Combine and heat ingredients; add 1 tablespoon cornstarch mixed with 1 tablespoon water.

Tip

Don't throw away that sweet pickle, dill pickle, or olive juice. Save it to add to mayonnaise (1 cup mayonnaise to 2 tablespoons pickle juice), chili sauce, or cream sauces for a new taste experience.

CLARIFIED BUTTER

Clarified butter is a special delicacy over asparagus, fresh peas, etc. It is similar to the Indian ghee.

Slowly melt butter in a pan that is deeper than wide. Skim off foam and save. Pour off clear melted fluid carefully, leaving the cloudy material in the bottom of the pan. Use the foam you have skimmed off and the cloudy matter from the bottom of the pan to flavor rice or mashed potatoes. Clarified butter will keep longer than whole butter.

SOUPS

MADELINE TEETSELL'S SORREL SOUP

2 cups sorrel (trim stems off)
2 tablespoons butter
2 tablespoons flour
1½ teaspoons salt
1 quart boiling water

2 cups diced potatoes
1 pint sour cream or 1 cup butter-
    milk
Cubes of pimiento

Wash sorrel and trim stems off. In pot put butter and sorrel. Simmer until melted. Add flour and salt. Stir. Add boiling water and potatoes. Cook on low until potatoes are tender. Add sour cream or buttermilk. This improves if refrigerated· overnight. Heat soup slowly in top of double boiler. You can dot the soup with tiny cubes of pimiento for color when served. Serves 6.

Sorrel is a wild "weed." The largest leaves are found in organically rich, moist, sunny spots. Seeds of "French" sorrel may be purchased.

SORREL SOUP

Two cups chopped sorrel leaves, 2 cups finely chopped potatoes. Scald sorrel and potatoes by pouring 6 cups very hot water over them. Save water. Put sorrel, some of the water, potatoes, and 2 tablespoons butter with 1 teaspoon salt into blender. Whirl until smooth. Heat mixture with remaining water slowly, stirring. Serve hot with sour cream and chopped wild onion tops or chives. This smooth soup can also be served cold.

BRAISED BONES TO USE FOR BEEF BROTH

Have deep iron skillet very hot; put in bones and brown them on all sides in ¼ cup salad oil. Your soup will have a much richer taste and color. When browned, place bones in large kettle. Cover with water, add an onion and some celery leaves, salt and pepper. Cook slowly for about 2 hours. Remove bones; cool; skim off fat. Now your stock is ready for soup or general cooking. Freeze some for future use.

Tip

Whenever consommé or bouillon cubes are called for, you can substitute your own beef or chicken stock.

KING'S CONSOMMÉ

6 cups clear beef broth (or bouillon)
4 peppercorns

3 whole cloves
2 bay leaves
¼ teaspoon grated lemon peel

Ten minutes before serving, combine all the ingredients. Heat to boiling. Simmer 1 or 2 minutes; strain. Have dishes of thinly sliced radishes, zucchini squash, water chestnuts or Jerusalem artichoke roots, green onions, tiny cubes of strong cheese, toasted chop suey noodles, avocado slices to float on top. Your guests can choose flavor and texture combinations.

PEG'S CORN CHOWDER

¼ cup finely chopped onions
2 cups milk
1 medium can cream-style corn
1 small can whole-kernel corn

Salt and pepper
¼ cup chopped parsley leaves or cress leaves

Simmer onions in a small amount of water until tender. Warm milk in top of a large double boiler (corn and milk scorch easily when heated directly on the stove); add onions and water to milk. Whirl cream-style corn in blender until quite smooth; add this and can of whole-kernel corn; stir well; add salt and pepper to taste. This should be a thick chowder. (If too thick, add more milk.) Serve hot with a liberal sprinkling of parsley or cress on top.

Tip

To make your own cream-style corn, with a sharp knife, slit down the center of each row of kernels and push out pulp and juice with dull edge of the knife.

THE FARM CLAM CHOWDER

1 pound salt pork
6 medium-sized white onions, finely chopped
5 medium-sized potatoes, diced
½ peck clams in shell

½ cup cornmeal
¼ teaspoon cracked black pepper
Salt to taste after cooking
2 quarts milk

Dice salt pork (cutting off rind) and brown in cast-iron Dutch oven. Remove pork dices from kettle and brown onions in fat from pork. Drain off fat; discard. Add to the onions in the pot the potatoes and water to cover. Clean sand from clams by covering them with water and adding ½ cup cornmeal. Leave for ½ hour before shucking. Rinse clams under tap and set aside in clean pan to collect juices for ½ hour. Shuck clams, adding juices to chowder pot. Mince clams, add and season. Add milk. Cook over medium heat for ¾ hour. Serve hot with dry crackers.

COOL SUMMER SOUP

1 large onion, chopped
2 cups chicken broth
2½ cups yellow summer squash, chopped fine
1 cup carrots, chopped fine
1 cup whole kernel corn

¼ teaspoon crumbled dried basil leaves
Salt and pepper
½ cup milk
Chopped parsley
Toasted sunflower seeds or almonds

Sauté onion in butter or margarine, add half of broth, squash, carrots, and corn; simmer 10 minutes. Mix in blender at medium speed ½ at a time until smooth and creamy. Add basil, salt and pepper to taste; chill. When ready to serve, stir in milk, balance of broth; sprinkle parsley and nuts on top.

DESSERTS

FOURTH OF JULY ICE CREAM

Every Fourth we get out our White Mountain ice-cream freezer. It takes no expensive energy—just elbow grease—and it is fun for everyone!

Buy about 3 pounds rock salt—might be well to buy a large bag for winter use (houseperson should hide about 3 pounds for this celebration). For about two weeks prior to the Fourth, fill any large plastic container with water and put into you freezer. If you have only one big container, fill, freeze solid, empty into freezer, fill with water, and repeat process. If you are lucky, you may live near a bulk ice plant and may be able to buy about 25 pounds of ice. (The cubes sold in machines get pretty expensive for this use.)

When ready to freeze ice cream, place ice in canvas or burlap bag and break it with a hammer into pieces which will fit in the ice-cream freezer. Following are some of our ice-cream recipes.

PEG'S ICE-CREAM BASE (FRENCH VANILLA)

½ cup sugar
¼ teaspoon salt
4 egg yolks, slightly beaten
2 cups scalded milk

2 cups heavy cream
2 cups half-and-half
1 tablespoon vanilla

Mix sugar, salt, and egg yolks; pour into milk in top of double boiler, stirring constantly. Cook until mixture coats spoon. Cool. (If lumpy, use wire whisk to beat smooth.) Add heavy cream, half-and-half, and vanilla. If you wish a fruit ice cream, add 8 fresh peaches, peeled and sliced, or 3 cups sliced fresh strawberries. Put into gallon freezer can to about ¾ full. (See Appendix, page 246, for freezer source.) Serves 12.

ICE-CREAM TOPPINGS

Whirl in blender ¼ cup dry ground coffee. Pour crème de cacao or coffee liqueur over ice cream; top with the pulverized ground coffee. Or, in blender, place a cup of apricot preserves, a tablespoon of lemon juice, and three mint leaves; mix well. Try adding enough creme de menthe to color and flavor one small bottle of light corn syrup.

RICH CHOCOLATE ICE CREAM (for ½-gallon hand freezer)

6 ounces cooking chocolate
1¼ cups sugar
½ cup boiling water
3 cups milk
2 tablespoons flour

3 egg yolks
½ teaspoon salt
1 cup heavy cream
1 tablespoon vanilla

Melt chocolate over hot water (in a double boiler); add one cup of sugar and boiling water and stir and cook directly over the fire until smooth and boiling. Scald milk; stir flour into milk until smooth; stir until milk thickens; then add the chocolate mixture, cover, and let cook 15 minutes. Beat the yolks of eggs; add salt and ¼ cup sugar. Beat again and stir into the hot mixture; stir until the egg is cooked a little; add heavy cream and strain into the can of the freezer. When cold, add vanilla. Freeze as usual. Double for gallon freezer.

ECONOMY RICH ICE CREAM

Follow directions, except substitute for 1 cup heavy cream, 1 cup powdered milk mixed in 1 cup water.

For 6 ounces of chocolate: 1 cup cocoa and ½ teaspoon instant coffee. This is excellent and lower in calories and cost than the original recipe.

VIRGINIA'S DEVIL'S FOOD CUSTARD CAKE

Prepare the following custard. Cook and stir in a saucepan over a very low flame

4 ounces baking chocolate   1 cup light brown sugar
½ cup milk   1 egg yolk

Keep custard below boiling point. Remove from fire when thick and smooth. Cool.

1 cup white sugar, sifted
½ cup butter, beaten until soft

Add sugar gradually. Blend these ingredients until very light and creamy. Beat in 2 egg yolks one at a time.

Sift before measuring—2 cups flour. Resift with 1 teaspoon soda and ½ teaspoon salt. Add flour to butter mixture in 3 parts alternately with thirds of

¼ cup water
½ cup milk
 1 teaspoon vanilla

After each addition, beat batter until smooth. Stir in custard. Whip 2 egg whites until stiff but not dry. Fold them lightly into the cake batter. Bake the cake in three greased 9-inch layer pans in a moderate oven (375º) for about 25 minutes. Spread with chocolate icing or 7-minute icing.

MARGARET KING'S SPONGE CAKE

4 eggs
3 tablespoons cold water
1 cup sugar
1½ tablespoons cornstarch
    Sifted cake flour

1¼ teaspoons baking powder
½ teaspoon salt
1 teaspoon flavoring, vanilla, lemon, or almond

Separate whites and yolks of eggs. Beat yolks in large bowl with cold water until thick and lemon colored. Add sugar gradually, beating each time a little is added. Put cornstarch in measuring cup and fill cup with sifted cake flour. Put into sifter and add baking powder and salt before sifting. Sift together. Add sifted dry ingredients to egg mixture and beat hard. Add flavoring and last, fold in stiffly beaten egg whites. Bake about 30 minutes in greased and floured sponge cake pan. Start oven at 375º. After about 10 minutes reduce heat to 350º. If you have the pans, this recipe makes excellent ladyfingers. Reduce cooking time to 15 or 20 minutes. We sometimes add a tablespoon of finely grated lemon or orange peel.

Tip

<u>To prepare loaf cake or sponge or fruitcake pans, do not grease bottoms, but line bottom with waxed paper (heavy), grease the paper and sides, dust with flour. Grease and flour tube if using tubular pan.</u>

BLUEBERRY TEA CAKE

Little Miss Delano of the alert mind and bright sparkling eyes always walked with a cane. She was my grandmother's friend, and when we went to tea she would tell us about Indian times in the area around Freetown, Massachusetts. Punctuating any conversation was, "Now, let me give you a pointer!" accompanied by small thumps of her cane. Because she was a staunch Republican, she was embarrassed by her relationship to FDR, who was then president. Here is her tea cake, always served with a mysterious and delicate tea.

2 cups sifted flour
2 teaspoons baking powder
½ teaspoon salt
¼ cup butter or margarine
¾ cup sugar

1 unbeaten egg
½ cup milk
2 cups blueberries lightly dusted with flour

Sift dry ingredients together; cream butter or margarine and sugar; add egg and milk and beat until smooth. Add dry ingredients, then fold in blueberries. Place in greased 9-inch by 9-inch pan.

CRUMB TOPPING

Mix together

½ cup sugar
¼ cup flour

½ teaspoon cinnamon
¼ cup butter or margarine, melted

Sprinkle cake with topping and bake at 375⁰ for 35 to 40 minutes or until it looks done.

EMILY KING'S CHEESECAKE (BRÛLEÉ)

18 half graham crackers

⅓ cup melted butter

Roll and mix; line bottom of springform pan.

2 8-ounce packages cream cheese, softened
3 eggs

¾ cup sugar
Juice of 1 lemon

Mix until smooth and pour into the shell; bake 20 minutes in 350° oven. Cool completely.

Mix

1 pint sour cream

½ cup granulated sugar

¾ teaspoon vanilla

Pour above mixture over cool cake. Bake for 5 minutes in 500° oven. Keep in refrigerator 24 hours or overnight.

Tips

Dried-out cake can be made into crumbs that may be used where graham cracker crumbs are called for; use the same method as for bread crumbs.

I've just remembered that my mother used to use a clean dishcloth, dipped in cold water and wrung out, to release a cake from a cake pan. Place cloth on bottom of hot cake pan. Almost infallible.

Dried cake can always be steamed with a lemon sauce or hard sauce. It will make a delicious dessert.

PEG'S MOTHER'S FRUITCAKE (from Mrs. Kingsbury)

In late October, there were fragrant doings in our kitchen at home as the Christmas fruitcake was being made. Here it is:

One pound fat salt pork chopped fine; pour over it 1 pint boiling water. Let stand until cool. Then add 1½ cups brown sugar and 2 eggs.

Dissolve 1 tablespoon soda in 2 cups molasses. Add this along with

1 tablespoon each cinnamon and cloves
1 pound each seeded raisins and currants (I use seedless raisins)

1 cup each citron, orange peel, lemon peel, figs, and dates
7 cups flour, sifted before measuring (I add 1 teaspoon baking powder)

Use loaf or angel cake ring pans. (Prepare pans as given in tip, page 154.)

Fill only half full. Bake in moderate oven for 3 hours. Remove cakes from oven, allow to cool thoroughly. Remove from pans. Waxed paper will come out of pans with the cake and should be peeled off just before using. These cakes were then "put down" in a clean, covered wash boiler in a cool place to age until ready to use.

How I remember this now! We children seeded the big, fat, sticky raisins, separated the citron, helped make the orange and lemon peel, and most fun of all were the turns we took at mixing the big canning kettle of batter. These cakes were given as gifts, served to the frequent guests for tea and at mother's very special New Year's Day open house. Such beautiful memories!

MOCHA TORTE

TORTE

2 cups shelled walnuts or pecans   6 egg whites
1½ cups sifted confectioners'
        sugar

Cover 2 cookie sheets with brown paper and trace the outline of two loaf pans on each sheet. Oil or grease inside the lines. Sprinkle with flour. Set oven at 350°.

Grind nuts in rotary grinder and mix thoroughly with confectioners' sugar. Beat egg whites until very stiff. Gently fold in nuts and sugar.

With long metal spatula smooth mixture into the pan outlines. Bake 30 to 35 minutes (it is important that tortes still be soft when removed from the oven). Cool until firm enough to slide the very fragile tortes carefully off the paper onto racks.

FROSTING

½ cup butter
1½ cups confectioners' sugar
1 teaspoon vanilla extract
1 tablespoon instant coffee

4 egg yolks
1 square bitter chocolate
Whole nuts

Work butter until creamy. Add sugar and beat until smooth. Add vanilla and coffee and beat in egg yolks. Add rotary-grated bitter chocolate. Shortly before dinner spread frosting between layers and on top of torte. Decorate with whole nuts. Serves 8.

HANOVER BICENTENNIAL CHERRY "CAKE"

1½ cups sifted all-purpose flour
1 teaspoon baking powder
¼ teaspoon salt
¼ cup sugar

¼ cup butter or margarine, melted
1 egg, beaten
½ teaspoon vanilla extract

Preheat oven to 350⁰. Sift flour, baking powder, salt, and sugar into a mixing bowl. Using a pastry blender, blend in the butter or margarine until it resembles a coarse cornmeal. Add the egg and vanilla. Mix until the dough sticks together in a ball. Line bottom of 9-inch by 13-inch pan. Prick pastry with a fork to prevent puffing while baking. Bake at 350° until golden color and firm to touch, about 10 to 15 minutes.

TOPPING

1 No. 2 can pie cherries, drained, saving juice (or use 2 cups cooked sour cherries)
½ cup sugar
¼ cup water
2 tablespoons cornstarch
Dash of salt
½ teaspoon almond extract

Put cherry juice, salt, and sugar in a saucepan and bring to a boil. Mix water and cornstarch and add to boiling cherry juice. Cook 2 minutes, stirring constantly. Add cherries and almond extract. Pour over baked crust. Serve with whipped cream when cool.

JACK-O'-LANTERN PIE OR CUSTARD MIX

The day before Halloween, when the family carves the jack-o'-lantern, remember to save the seeds for you and the birds. Discard the stringy matter, but scrape out as much of the meat as the pumpkin carvers will have patience to wait for. The day after Halloween, grab that pumpkin and any others you can, and make up this recipe multiplied by seven to freeze uncooked, ready to make into cup custards or pies during the winter. Make your packages single-pie size and so mark them.

1½ cups cooked and mashed pumpkin	1 tablespoon molasses
1 cup evaporated milk	1 teaspoon cinnamon
3 eggs, beaten	1 teaspoon ginger
1 cup firmly packed brown sugar	⅛ teaspoon ground allspice
	½ teaspoon salt

PIE

Preheat oven 400°. Combine all ingredients; pour into chilled pastry shell; bake for 40 minutes, or until knife inserted near edge of pie comes out clean. Cool on wire rack. Makes one 9-inch pie.

CUSTARD

You may also cook this mix as a baked custard. Place mix in buttered baking dish. Set dish in shallow pan of water. Bake at 350° until knife inserted comes out clean.

CHOCOLATE CHIFFON PIE (filling for one 9-inch pie)

1 envelope gelatin
6 level tablespoons cocoa or 2
   squares bitter chocolate
1 cup sugar
3 eggs, separated

¼ teaspoon salt
1 teaspoon vanilla
   Baked pie shell or graham cracker
   crust
   Whipped cream (optional)

Soften gelatin in ¼ cup cold water. Put ½ cup cold water in top of double boiler; add cocoa or bitter chocolate. When thoroughly dissolved, add ½ cup sugar, then egg yolks slightly beaten, and salt. Cook until custard consistency, stirring constantly. Add softened gelatin to hot custard and stir until dissolved. Cool and add vanilla. When mixture begins to thicken, fold in stiffly beaten egg whites to which the other ½ cup sugar has been added. Fill baked pie shell or graham cracker crust and chill. Just before serving, a thin layer of whipped cream may be spread over the pie.

LINDY'S STRAWBERRY PIE

When we were newly married and lived in Greenwich Village, our entertainment was often a long walk on New York's streets. One summer evening, we stood in front of Lindy's Restaurant and were tempted inside by the sight of a fabulous strawberry pie on display. Fabulous it was. This is our approximation of the recipe.

1 8-oz. package cream cheese
   Sour cream or buttermilk
1 teaspoon powdered sugar
1 box strawberries
   (save 4 large berries to
   decorate with)

¼ cup sugar
2 tablespoons cornstarch
½ teaspoon almond extract

Using ½ Flaky Pie Crust recipe (page 180), line the bottom of a 9-inch pie pan. Prick bottom and cook until light brown. Cool. Soften cream cheese with sour cream until just able to spread, and mix in powdered sugar. Line cool pie crust with this mixture. Slice strawberries in sugar; toss; let stand until juices start to come out. Remove a small amount of juice and mix with cornstarch and almond extract. Mix cornstarch thickening with strawberries; put over low fire; cook, stirring constantly until quite thick. Set aside to cool, then fill pie shell with strawberry mixture. Top with saved strawberries, halved, and refrigerate before serving.

LEMON MERINGUE PIE

4 tablespoons cornstarch
1¼ cups sugar
1 cup lemon juice
1 tablespoon grated lemon rind

3 eggs, separated
¾ cup boiling water
½ Flaky Pie Crust recipe (page 180)

Combine cornstarch, sugar, lemon juice, and lemon rind. Beat egg yolks; add cornstarch mixture. Gradually add boiling water. Heat to boiling over direct heat and then boil gently for 4 minutes, stirring constantly. Pour into baked pie shell.

MERINGUE

Beat 3 egg whites until stiff, but not dry. Gradually add 6 tablespoons sugar. Spread meringue over top of pie, carefully sealing in all of the filling by spreading meringue to touch all edges of crust. Bake in a hot oven (425º) 4 to 5 minutes or until brown.

Tips

Too much sugar in meringues will make them watery.

Boots Bruner adds this tip. Before beating egg whites, add ¼ teaspoon baking powder to them. You will have a higher meringue.

WHEN PERSIMMONS ARE RIPE

Persimmon recipes are hard to find. To prepare persimmons for use, scoop out pulp, discarding seeds and skin; whirl in blender. For each 2 cups of pulp add 1 tablespoon lemon juice. This prepared pulp may be frozen for future use.

PERSIMMON CHIFFON PIE

Preheat oven to 425°. Prepare ½ Flaky Pie Crust recipe (page 180), but add ¼ cup finely chopped almonds or pecans. Line a 9-inch pie pan; prick bottom of pastry; bake for 10 to 15 minutes at 425°, remove and cool.

FILLING

1 envelope unflavored gelatin
¼ cup cold water
1½ cups prepared persimmon
    pulp (see above)
1 teaspoon grated lemon rind

¼ cup lemon juice
10 tablespoons sugar
3 egg whites
1 cup whipping cream

Soften gelatin in cold water in top of double boiler for 10 minutes; place over warm water and stir till dissolved. Combine persimmon pulp, lemon rind and juice, and 4 tablespoons sugar in a bowl. Add gelatin and mix well;

chill until it begins to thicken. Beat egg whites until they froth, then add the remaining sugar, 1 tablespoon at a time, beating hard between each addition. Whip cream. Divide in half. Fold egg whites and ½ the cream alternately into the persimmon mix. Place in pie crust. Spread remaining whipped cream on top of pie.

PEG'S PECAN PIE

3 tablespoons soft butter or margarine
½ cup dark brown sugar
½ cup light corn syrup
1 teaspoon vanilla

¾ cup coarsely chopped pecans
3 eggs
1 9-inch pie shell, unbaked (see page 180)
¼ cup pecan halves

Preheat oven to 375°. Cream together butter or margarine and brown sugar until very smooth; add corn syrup, vanilla, and chopped pecans. Beat eggs until very fluffy, and very gently turn into other ingredients. Pour into unbaked pie shell; top with remaining pecan halves in a flower or other design. Bake at 375° for 30 to 40 minutes, or until a knife comes out clean. Cool and serve.

CRANBERRY CHEESE PIE

2½ 8-ounce packages (20 ounces) cream cheese
1 cup sugar
1½ tablespoons flour
¼ teaspoon grated lemon rind
¼ teaspoon grated orange rind
⅛ teaspoon salt
3 eggs
1 egg white
2 tablespoons evaporated or homogenized milk
½ teaspoon vanilla
1 9-inch pie shell, slightly underbaked (see page 180)
1-pound can whole cranberry sauce
2 tablespoons sugar
1 tablespoon cornstarch
1 teaspoon lemon juice
1 teaspoon grated lemon rind

Preheat oven to 450⁰. Whip cream cheese until fluffy. Combine sugar, flour, ¼ teaspoon grated lemon rind, grated orange rind, and ⅛ teaspoon salt. Add to the cream cheese and beat until thoroughly mixed. Add eggs one at a time and then egg white, beating well after each addition. Add evaporated or homogenized milk and vanilla, beating again until well blended.

Pour into slightly underbaked 9-inch pie shell. Bake 7 minutes in a very hot oven, 450⁰. Reduce to a slow oven, 200⁰, and bake 15 minutes more. Cool.

Prepare a topping by combining in a saucepan cranberry sauce, sugar, and cornstarch. Cook over low heat until thick and clear. Blend in lemon juice and 1 teaspoon grated lemon rind. Cool and spread over the cooled cheese filling.

DEEP DISH PEAR PIE (SECKEL PEARS)

PEAR FILLING

2 pounds (about 18) Seckel pears   Dash of salt
1 tablespoon lemon juice   ½ teaspoon cinnamon
3 tablespoons flour   ½ teaspoon nutmeg
1 cup sugar   1 tablespoon butter or margarine

Peel pears; cut in halves and core. Arrange in 1½-quart baking dish. Sprinkle with lemon juice. Mix flour, sugar, salt, and spices together and sprinkle over pears. Dot with butter.

PASTRY

1 cup sifted all-purpose flour   ⅓ cup shortening
½ teaspoon salt   ¼ cup grated Cheddar cheese

Preheat oven to 350°. Sift flour and salt together; cut in shortening with a pastry blender until mixture looks like coarse cornmeal. Mix in the cheese; stir in water, a tablespoon at a time until pastry holds together. Chill in refrigerator for about 1 hour. Roll pastry out in a circle a little larger than the top of the baking dish. Slash in several places and arrange over pears, crimping pastry to edges of dish securely. Bake 30 to 40 minutes. Serve with cream or sour cream.

LEMON SPONGE PIE

1 tablespoon butter
2 tablespoons flour
1 cup sugar
2 egg yolks, beaten

2 egg whites, stiffly beaten
Juice and grated rind of
  1 lemon
1 cup milk

Mix butter, flour, and sugar together. Add eggs, lemon juice and grated rind, then milk. Bake in uncooked pie shell at 300° for approximately 20 to 30 minutes.

GREEN TOMATO MINCEMEAT

Chop fine 4 quarts green tomatoes; drain and cover with cold water. Boil 30 minutes and drain. Add 4 quarts peeled, chopped apples, 2 pounds brown sugar, 1 pound seeded raisins, ¼ pound citron, ½ cup chopped suet, 1 teaspoon salt, ½ cup vinegar.

Stir well; cook until thick. When cold, add ½ teaspoon cloves, 1 teaspoon each of cinnamon and nutmeg.

Dessert Tips

When recipe calls for grated orange peel, try lemon, lime, or grapefruit peel for variety.

Always rinse, with cold water, a pan in which you plan to heat milk; less chance of scorching.

In gelatin desserts, we always substitute a compatible fruit juice for the water called for.

Save orange and lemon peels. Dry them thoroughly, whirl in blender until pulverized, or grate fine. Use as flavorings in cakes and puddings.

My mother said to put a pinch of salt in all desserts even it not called for. It heightens flavor.

Any chocolate used is greatly improved in flavor by adding a pinch of instant coffee.

Three tablespoons of strong tea with a pinch of nutmeg adds an interesting flavor to apple pie.

Nutmegs should be grated at the blossom end first.

Grease your spoon or cup when measuring syrup, molasses, or honey, and the sticky substance will roll right off.

Since there is considerable question about the safety of red food coloring, consider this: Wash 4 beets carefully; boil whole until done, in about a cup to a cup and a half of water. Drain, saving water. Use beets for a salad or hot vegetable. Use water for food coloring, boiling down to desired depth of color. Because of beets' mild sweetness, this color can be used in cakes and candies.

You may also color your cakes and candies with blueberry or grape juice.

When cooking fruits which must have sugar added, such as applesauce or cranberries, cook fruit first then add sugar to taste. Far less sugar is used this way.

Substitute honey for granulated sugar whenever you can.

To cool a watermelon when the refrigerator is full, cut watermelon meat into sticks. Remove seeds and cool sticks in refrigerator in quart canning jars.

For a topping for hot desserts, whip 1 large package of cream cheese with 3 tablespoons milk and 1 tablespoon honey or sugar.

LEMON OR GRAPEFRUIT GELATIN DESSERT

2 packages unflavored gelatin
2 cups lemon or grapefruit juice
⅔ cup honey
¼ teaspoon salt
½ cup boiling water

Dissolve gelatin in 1 cup lemon or grapefruit juice over low flame. Add rest of ingredients. Last to go in is the boiling water. Let set and chill.

COFFEE DESSERT

Same as above, only in place of water and juice use strong, black coffee. Use sugar instead of honey.

CITRUS CURD

4 eggs
1 cup sugar
½ cup lime, lemon, orange, or grapefruit juice
1 teaspoon lime or lemon rind, grated
¼ pound soft butter or margarine

Beat eggs until light; mix in sugar, juice, and rind. Place in top of double boiler. Add butter, place over hot water, and cook, stirring constantly, until filling becomes thick as mayonnaise. Remove from heat; let cool, then chill. Use in tart shells or on French toast or pancakes.

For a luncheon fresh-fruit salad or compote, mix 2 tablespoons dry mustard with 1 cup sugar to 1 quart fruit and their juices.

We keep a shaker-top spice bottle handy with a mixture of cinnamon and sugar to use for pies, cookies, toast.

Add a pinch of salt and a few drops of vanilla to fruit cup.

A dash of almond extract added to any stone fruit dessert adds interest. Stone fruits: peaches, apricots, plums, cherries, persimmons.

For a quick dessert, split banana lengthwise, top with whipped cream and bitter chocolate curls.

FLORENCE CUTTING'S APPLE CRISP

6 large apples   Juice of 1 lemon

Mix together

1 cup graham cracker crumbs   Dash of salt
1 cup brown sugar   ½ teaspoon cinnamon
½ cup white sugar   ½ teaspoon nutmeg
1 tablespoon grated orange or lem-   Moisten with ½ cup melted
   on peel   butter or margarine

    Grease a 9-inch by 9-inch by 2-inch pan; peel and core apples and slice into bottom of pan. Sprinkle with crumb mixture and juice of 1 lemon. Bake at 350º for 45 minutes.

Tip

Bread crumbs can easily be made from stale bread or leftover morning toast. Lay slices on a cookie tin to dry and when something comes out of the oven and while there is still heat in the oven, slip your bread in to dry to a crisp. A quick whirl in the blender will give you bread crumbs which can be stored for a month or more in the refrigerator, indefinitely in the freezer.

STEAMED ORANGE PUDDING (USING BREAD CRUMBS)

¾ cup scalded milk
½ cup bread crumbs
1 tablespoon butter, melted
2 eggs

¼ cup sugar
Grated rind and juice of
   ½ orange
1 tablespoon lemon juice
2 tablespoons chopped almonds

Pour the milk over the crumbs and butter and let stand for an hour. Beat the eggs; add sugar and beat again. Add grated orange rind, fruit juices, and almonds; mix all together. Place in covered casserole in 350° oven for 45 minutes. Serve with hard sauce, bitter chocolate sauce, or hot dessert topping.

BLUEBERRY DAYS

When I was a young girl and used to go high-bush blueberrying with my father, this dessert was the reward at the end of a long day's picking. The other rewards of the warm July days were the long talks and equally long silences with my father as we shared an enjoyable summer day, picked the big, blue, perfect berries hanging in full clusters above our heads, and listened to the catbirds scold us for stealing their store.

BLUEBERRY PUDDING WITH BLUEBERRY HARD SAUCE—ENJOY!!

BLUEBERRY HARD SAUCE (MAKE AHEAD)

5 tablespoons butter
¾ cup sugar
1 teaspoon vanilla

1 pinch salt
1 cup blueberries

Cream butter; add sugar gradually, creaming until light and fluffy. Add vanilla and salt; mix thoroughly; pour in blueberries. Mix by hand until some berries are mashed and some still whole. Serves 5 to 6.

BLUEBERRY PUDDING

2 cups flour
2 teaspoons baking powder
½ teaspoon salt
1 cup sugar

1 tablespoon butter
1 cup milk
1 cup blueberries

Sift flour, baking powder, and salt; cream sugar and butter. Mix all ingredients together except blueberries. Shake blueberries with only enough flour to coat them (keeps berries from all going to the bottom). Add coated berries to mixture and place in buttered casserole for about 40 minutes at 350º. Serve hot with hard sauce.

CRANBERRY DAYS

When Ted and I lived in New Hampshire, we used to save the first week in October for a weekend trip to The Farm in Massachusetts where my parents would be holding onto the last warm days of summer before returning to our home in Upper Montclair, New Jersey. On a crisp, clear day we would drive the half mile to the nearby cranberry bog. We would be laden with 10-quart pails and bushel boxes. It was owned by Mr. DeSilva, a Portuguese cranberry farmer, who had bought a swamp years earlier from my grandmother. He turned the swamp into a series of planted squares marked off by narrow water channels which were used in flooding the bog in the winter. The sky would be the deepest, clearest blue, the bog stretching before us was of a deep scarlet touched with burgundy. The pickers had done their work days before and we were the gleaners. We took home bushels of cranberries which we enjoyed all winter. They keep very well covered with water or even dry in a box stored in a cool place.

After our Cranberry Days we would return to the farmhouse (built in 1724), and before a roaring applewood fire in the fireplace with its crane, we would sort cranberries and talk.

CRANBERRY PUDDING

Use cranberries instead of blueberries, but cook cranberries just until they pop. Drain off some juice, allow to cool, then add cooked cranberries to hard sauce. Substitute 1 cup chopped, uncooked cranberries for the blueberries in the blueberry pudding recipe.

HARD SAUCES—SOME FLAVOR COMBINATIONS

Lemon hard sauce over vanilla- or chocolate-flavored dishes. Almond hard sauce over stone fruit desserts, i.e., peach, apricot, plum. Mint hard sauce over chocolate, lemon, lime, or pear dessert. Of course, hard sauce is at its best over a piping hot dessert.

CRANBERRY PANCAKES

Sift together
1½ cups flour
1 teaspoon salt

½ cup sugar
2½ teaspoons baking powder

Beat lightly

2 eggs

Add

3 tablespoons melted butter   1 cup milk

   Make a hole in the center of the dry ingredients. Pour in the liquid ingredients. Stir quickly until just blended. Now add 1 cup fresh cranberries
that have been washed and cut in half. This batter can be made the
night before. Just add the cranberries in the morning.

CRANBERRY SYRUP

2 cups water   1 cup cranberries
1½ cups sugar

   Combine and boil the above ingredients, stirring frequently for about 5
minutes. When cool, whirl in blender until smooth and creamy. This will
keep in the refrigerator for weeks or can be canned.

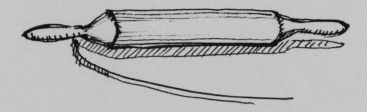

FLAKY PIE CRUST
(for 9-inch, 2-Crust pie)

Sift in bowl
2 cups sifted all-purpose flour   1½ teaspoons salt

Pour over the top all at once without mixing
½ cup salad oil   ¼ cup milk

Stir these ingredients lightly until blended. Form them into a ball. Divide ball into 2 parts. Flatten slightly. Roll the dough between sheets of waxed paper to desired thinness. Patch tears, if any, by sticking pieces of dough together. Proceed as with any pie crust. Bake in 400º oven for about 40 minutes. For 1 baked pie shell to be filled later, use ½ the ingredients. Bake in hot oven 475º about 10 minutes.

CLOVER JOHNSON'S MAPLE BAVARIAN CREAM

2 egg yolks
½ cup shaved maple sugar (or 1
    cup maple syrup—and reduce
    milk to ½ cup)
¼ teaspoon salt

1 cup milk
1 envelope gelatin
¼ cup cold water
½ teaspoon vanilla
1 cup cream, whipped

Beat egg yolks with maple sugar and salt, add to milk and cook in double boiler until of custard consistency. Soften gelatin in cold water. Add to hot custard and stir until dissolved. Cool, and when mixture begins to thicken, fold in vanilla and whipped cream. Turn into mold that has been rinsed in cold water and chill. When firm, unmold. Serves 6.

Tip

The whites of eggs, stiffly beaten, may be added to cream mixture if desired.

FRILLS
AND
THINGS

GINGER

Grow your own ginger and have an attractive houseplant to boot. The plant from which we obtain commercial ginger is called Zingiber of—ficinale. It is usually imported from India, West Africa, or the West Indies. Ginger is a graceful, bamboo-like plant. It forms fat tubers which are dug up, scrubbed clean, plunged into boiling water to prevent sprouting, dried, and then ground or candied in chunks after the tuber is peeled. You may use this same process to make your homegrown ginger. Ginger pays real dividends as a houseplant. Its leaves and stems are a graceful addition to a plant window—growing three to four feet tall and presenting you in the fall with small, orchid-like flowers of yellow-green with their lips spotted with dark purple and yellow. Root divisions are used to propagate this plant so do not feel bad about taking most of the tuber for eating ginger. Save enough root to start again. Rich soil, constant moisture, and semishade are needed to grow ginger. Alberts and Merkel will have Zingiber (see Appendix, page 246). Be sure to get Zingiber officinale, because there are other ornamental gingers whose roots are not useful for food.

MRS. ALLEN'S GINGER PUFFS

1 cup sugar
1 teaspoon cinnamon
3 teaspoons baking soda
2 cups flour
1 teaspoon ginger or ½ inch fat
   ginger root, chopped fine with
   skin on

¾ cup solid shortening
1 egg
5 tablespoons molasses

Preheat oven to 350°. Sift dry ingredients together (if using chopped ginger, add with molasses); combine all ingredients and mix well. Form into small marbles; roll in sugar. Bake 12 minutes on greased cookie sheet at 350°. If too stiff, add more molasses.

WONDERFUL BROWNIES

4 squares baking chocolate
½ cup melted butter
2 cups sugar
2 eggs, unbeaten

1½ teaspoons vanilla
1 cup flour
¼ teaspoon salt
1 cup nuts, chopped

Melt chocolate and butter in top of double boiler. Cool slightly and add rest of ingredients, mixing well. Bake in well-greased 9-inch by 9-inch cake pan at 350º for 30 minutes. Cut hot and remove from pan immediately.

AUNT CHATTIE'S COOKIES

2 egg whites, beaten stiff and dry
2 cups light brown sugar
2 cups pecans or walnuts, chopped

½ teaspoon salt
1 teaspoon vanilla
2 tablespoons flour

Mix egg whites and brown sugar. Dust pecans or walnuts with flour and add nuts salt, vanilla, and flour to egg and sugar. Drop by teaspoonfuls on a very well greased cookie sheet. Bake in 350º oven for 10 to 15 minutes. Allow to cool slightly before removing to wire rack to finish cooling. If cookies stick, return to oven for a minute.

KATHRYN SIBLEY'S SWISS SCHINDELN

1¼ cups shelled hazelnuts
6 egg whites
1 cup sugar

⅛ teaspoon salt
3 tablespoons all-purpose flour
1 teaspoon cinnamon

Start your oven at 350º or moderate and grease a cookie sheet thoroughly. Grate or grind nuts. We find that using a rotary grater makes nuts fine and fluffy. Now beat egg whites until they hold a point. Mix together grated nuts, sugar, salt, flour, and cinnamon and fold into the stiffly beaten egg whites. Mix until all ingredients are thoroughly combined. Do not over-mix.

Drop teaspoonfuls of batter onto baking sheet. With wet spatula smooth tops of cookies into very thin oval shapes. Keep even in thickness. Or drop on sheet in small mounds like a macaroon cookie. Bake 10 to 14 minutes or until edges brown. Remove from sheet immediately. Shape over rolling pin until cold. Makes 5 dozen. If you are making macaroon mounds, do not shape.

Tip
After cookies are baked, if you have trouble getting them off the sheet, reheat a minute or two in oven.

SCOTCH SHORTBREAD

½ pound butter
1 teaspoon vanilla

¾ cup sifted confectioners' sugar
2 cups white flour

Cream butter until soft. Add vanilla. Blend sugar in gradually. Mix flour into butter and sugar with the hands. Pat or roll out to about ⅓-inch thick-ness. Cut into small diamonds or rectangles. Bake on an ungreased sheet at 300º for 40 minutes or until cream color. Makes about 2 dozen cookies.

Tip
We sometimes roll the dough into logs about ⅓ inch thick and 2 inches long, and after baking, dip one end in unsweetened chocolate which has been melted in the top of a double boiler. Then we roll in finely chopped nuts or colored cookie decorations, put them on racks until chocolate hardens.

CANDIES FOR CHRISTMAS

When we were young we used to stuff dates, make fudge and our favorite Sweet Dainties for our Christmas candies.

SWEET DAINTIES

4 cups sugar
¼ teaspoon salt
1½ cups boiling water
4 envelopes gelatin
1 cup cold water
Red and green coloring (paste or liquid, nontoxic type)

1 teaspoon cinnamon extract (or wintergreen)
½ teaspoon peppermint extract
Powdered or fine granulated sugar

Heat sugar, salt, and boiling water to boiling point. Soften gelatin in cold water. Add to hot syrup and stir until dissolved. Boil slowly for 15 minutes. Remove from fire and divide into 2 equal parts. Color one part a delicate red and flavor with cinnamon extract; color the other part a delicate green and flavor with peppermint extract. Rinse two pans (about 8 inches by 4 inches) in cold water, pour in candy mixture to the depth of about ¾ inch, and put in a cool place (not refrigerator), allowing candy to thicken for at least 12 hours. With a wet knife, loosen around edges of pan, pull candy out on board lightly covered with powdered sugar. Cut into cubes and roll in powdered or fine granulated sugar.

Note: If lemon flavor is desired, add 3 tablespoons juice of lemon or 2 teaspoons lemon extract to one part of the candy and leave it uncolored. The candy may be made by using 10 drops of oil of cinnamon or cloves instead of the extract. This must be stirred into the mixture thoroughly while hot. Why not try your favorite herbs to season these candies for hors d'oeuvres?

BETTY SILVER'S HOT PEPPER JELLY

1 dozen hot peppers
1 tablespoon salt

1½ pounds sugar
1 pint vinegar

Chop peppers, sprinkle with salt, and let stand 3 to 4 hours. Rinse well. Cover with sugar and vinegar. Boil slowly until thick. Put in sterilized glasses and cover with paraffin. Makes 4 to 5 glasses. Use with meats and hors d'oeuvres.

Tip
Wear rubber gloves or use a silicone cream on your hands when preparing hot peppers. If you do not, your hands will be on fire for the next few days whenever you get them wet.

RED SWEET PEPPER MARMALADE

12 medium-sized red sweet pep-
    pers
 4 teaspoons whole allspice
 ½ teaspoon ground ginger
 2 cups chopped onions

2 cups vinegar
3 cups honey
4 teaspoons salt
1 lemon, sliced

Remove stems and seeds from peppers. Cover peppers with boiling water; let stand 5 minutes; drain. Repeat and drain well. Put through coarse blade of food chopper. Should measure about 4 cups. Tie spices in cloth bag, combine other ingredients, and boil all 30 minutes, stirring occasionally. Let stand overnight. Next day, bring to boil in large saucepan and simmer 10 minutes. Ladle boiling hot into sterilized ½-pint jars. Seal. Makes 6 ½-pint jars.

HOT AND SWEET PEPPER JELLY

1½ cups cider vinegar
¾ cup bell peppers (measure after cutting up fine)
¼ cup hot peppers (measure after cutting up fine)

6½ cups sugar
½ bottle fruit pectin

Put ½ cup vinegar into blender and add the peppers. Reduce to a fine puree. Strain through a fine cheesecloth, then pour into a large, flat-bottomed kettle; add rest of vinegar and sugar; stir constantly and bring to a full rolling boil. Remove from heat and cool 5 minutes; skim off foam. Add fruit pectin and pour into sterilized glasses; cover with paraffin. Use as tiny cubes on cream cheese hors d'oeuvres and with all meats.

PEG'S GINGER PEARS

193
FRILLS AND THINGS

9 pounds pears (it is best to use
  hard-ripe pears such as Kief-
  fer)

6 pounds sugar
4 lemons
3 ounces crystallized ginger

Peel, core and cut fruit in thin slices; mix pears and sugar (be sure pears are dry). Stir and boil till sugar forms syrup and fruit is clear; add grated rind of 2 lemons and juice of all 4, also ginger, cut up in small pieces, and simmer until thick. Put in sterilized jelly glasses or seal in pint jars. Approximately 18 glasses.

RIPE CUCUMBER SWEET PICKLE

So often cucumbers get ahead of you in your garden; this is a way to use your ripe cucumbers.

7 large or 9 small cucumbers
1 tablespoon salt
1 teaspoon powdered alum
2 quarts vinegar
1 pound brown sugar

1 whole cinnamon stick
1 tablespoon whole cloves
  Pinch of cayenne pepper
¼ cup raisins

Remove the cucumber skins and seeds; cut into cubes or sticks. Cover with water and add salt and powdered alum. Soak overnight. In the morning, drain, rinse, and drain again. Place vinegar and brown sugar in a deep pan. Make a small cheesecloth bag and place in it cinnamon stick, whole cloves, and cayenne pepper. Heat the vinegar, sugar, and spices. When syrup is hot, add cucumbers, a few at a time, with a few raisins. Boil until cucumbers look clear; remove spice bag; put into sterilized jars and seal.

Tips

For apple jelly, eat your apple and make jelly too. When you peel and core apples for pie or applesauce, wash apples thoroughly before peeling; save peels and cores. Place peels and cores in a large kettle with 2 cups of water. Bring to a boil, stirring to keep from sticking. Mash with potato masher when soft; put to drain in cheese-cloth jelly bag overnight. Use fruit pectin recipe for making apple jelly.

Save all paraffin from jelly glasses; rinse well and store in clean coffee can for reuse.

The delicate flavors of fruits and berries can be lost by overcooking, and in the case of a few, such as blackberries, cherries, and apricots, can be made unpleasant to the taste by overheating. When cooking fruit for jelly or jam, boil only long enough to extract the juices. If the pulp is to be used as in jam, use a food mill, rather than cooking, to obtain the best from your fruit.

PLUM CONSERVE

3 pints plums, stoned
2 pounds granulated sugar
1 pound seeded raisins
2 oranges, sliced thin—remove
  seeds

¼ pound nuts
½ bottle fruit pectin

Boil first 4 ingredients 15 minutes. Then add nuts, chopped. Boil 15 minutes more, watching carefully, as it burns quickly. Add fruit pectin; boil 1 minute and ladle into glasses.

PERSIMMON JAM

3½ cups prepared fruit (pulp plus
     lemon juice, page 165)
6½ cups (2 pounds, 14 ounces)
     sugar

½ bottle fruit pectin

Place fruit and sugar, mixed, over high heat, bringing to full rolling boil. Boil hard 1 minute, stirring constantly. Remove from heat; stir in fruit pectin at once. Skim off foam with metal spoon. Stir and skim for 5 minutes to cool slightly. Ladle into glasses; cover with ⅛-inch hot paraffin.

PEACH CHUTNEY

3½ pounds peaches	2 large cloves garlic, minced
4 ounces ginger root, peeled and diced	¾ cup lime juice
3½ cups sugar	¾ teaspoon ground ginger
1½ cups vinegar	1 pod chili, crushed
4 tablespoons steak sauce	½ cup seedless raisins
	1 cup chopped onions

Peel and slice peaches ¼ inch thick. Cover with brine, made with 2 tablespoons salt and 1 quart water, and let stand 24 to 36 hours. Drain. Cook ginger in water to cover until almost tender. Drain; reserve water. Mix 4 tablespoons of reserved ginger water, sugar, vinegar, steak sauce, and garlic. Bring to a boil. Add peaches. Cook slowly until peaches are clear. Remove peaches from syrup; add cooked ginger and remaining ingredients. Cook until onions are soft and mixture is thickness desired. Return peaches to syrup. Return to heat; bring to a boil. Pour into hot, sterilized jars; seal. Yield 2½ pints.

Note: Ginger root is available in Chinese food stores and some supermarkets. Though less potent, crystallized ginger may be substituted. Soak it in water to cover until sugar crystals dissolve; dice. Use soaking water as a substitute for that in which the ginger root is cooked.

MAKING INSTANT COCOA IN QUANTITY

2½ cups sugar
¾ of a 16-ounce can of cocoa
1 16-ounce jar dry coffee cream
    substitute

1 14-quart box instant, nonfat, dry
    milk

Combine all ingredients and sift 10 times. Store in 2-pound coffee tins or large plastic containers. Use 2 teaspoons to a cup of boiling water.

OUR SUMMER COFFEE

For a stimulating summer drink, freeze very strong coffee (or add some instant coffee to your regular brew) in ice cube trays. Fill a tall glass with the cubes and pour warm milk over them. A dollop of whipped cream on top makes this an elegant drink. Serve straws or hollow iced tea spoons with this.

Tip
Iced tea ready all summer! We use a half-gallon jug filled with boiling water; at the jug's top we hang 4 teabags, held in place by the cap put on loosely. Let this steep until water is cool. Remove bags and refrigerate the

tea. Or, use cold water instead of hot; place outdoors in full sun for 4 to 5 hours.

To an 8-cup pot of coffee, add 1 teaspoon butter and 1 tablespoon cocoa. Mix cocoa with a little cold water before adding so that it will not be lumpy. A New Drink!

Keep skins of lemons after the juice has been squeezed out. Put as many as possible in a large jar and fill jar with water, cover, and refrigerate overnight. Use liquid, sweetened to taste, for a very nice drink.

LEMONADE BASE

1 tablespoon grated lemon peel
½ cup boiling water

1½ cups sugar
1½ cups lemon juice

Combine lemon peel, boiling water, and sugar. Stir until sugar is dissolved; cool. Add lemon juice. Mix well. Store in refrigerator until ready to use. Makes 2½ cups syrup.

By the glass: Pour ¼ cup syrup base into tall glass and add ¾ cup water and ice. Stir. By the pitcher: Combine full recipe with 5 cups cold water.

Tip

Simple syrup: Combine equal parts of sugar and water; cook until sugar dissolves. Keep a jar always handy for use in fruit drinks, iced tea and coffee, and in cooking fruit, or for serving over fresh fruit. Saves sugar. To keep fruits from darkening, bathe them in 1 cup simple syrup with 1 tablespoon lemon juice added.

GUACAMOLE

4 avocados, mashed and pureed
1 teaspoon salt
2 tablespoons lemon or lime juice
½ teaspoon steak sauce
⅛ teaspoon hot pepper sauce
1 medium tomato, chopped fine

Combine all ingredients thoroughly and chill. Serve on crackers or thin with sour cream for a dip.

SHRIMP SPREAD FOR A LARGE PARTY

3 pounds raw shrimp, cooked and
    cut in small pieces

Whip the following ingredients with eggbeater

2 large packages cream cheese
1 cup mayonnaise
1 cup sour cream
2 tablespoons celery, chopped very
  fine
1 tablespoon chopped green pepper

2 tablespoons grated onion
2 lemons, juice and grated rind
  Hot pepper sauce, paprika, and
    salt to taste

After the base is thoroughly mixed with beater, add cut-up shrimp and mix with wooden spoon. Serves 40.

MAKE YOUR OWN

OUR HOMEMADE PEANUT BUTTER

2 cups shelled peanuts   ¼ cup vegetable oil
½ teaspoon salt

If you are using raw peanuts, remove shells and put peanuts on a cookie sheet and roast in a 300° oven for ½ hour, turning them occasionally.

When cooked, cool. Without removing the skins, put in blender with the salt and start blender at low speed; pour in oil gradually until it is all used up, stopping occasionally to push peanuts down with rubber spatula. Keep whirling until you get the consistency you like; the less whirling, the crunchier.

We keep it in a jar in the refrigerator.

MEG'S HERB VINEGARS

When you have fresh herbs available, buy a gallon of good cider vinegar (or make your own—see From Cider to Vinegar, page 211). Sterilize pint screw-top canning jars. Wash thoroughly a large sprig or small bunch of any of the following: rosemary, summer or perennial savory, tarragon, thyme, sweet basil, dill, mint, oregano, sage or bay leaves, or marjoram. (See page 86, Cleaning Fresh Vegetables.) Place sprig or small bunch of fresh herb in jar. Fill with vinegar; screw tops on tightly. Do not try to pack herbs in. A little fresh herb goes a long way. Do not mix the herbs, since it is better to mix the herb vinegars after they are ready to use. Be sure to use coated jar tops—the vinegar will eat through exposed metal during storage. Store in cool, dark place. Seasoned vinegars should be ready in about 2 months, and will keep for at least a year. Discard herb after using vinegar. You can mix the various flavors to taste.

VIRGINIA'S SALAD SALT

1 jar onion salt
1 jar garlic salt
1 jar celery salt
1 jar savory salt
½ can paprika

16 rounded teaspoons salt
10 teaspoons sugar
½ teaspoon dry mustard
½ teaspoon black pepper

Mix well in a bowl. Store in glass jar. Use as needed.

MAKE YOUR OWN POULTRY SEASONING

¼ cup crumbled dried oregano
  leaves
½ cup crumbled dried thyme
  leaves
 1 cup crumbled dried sage leaves
¼ cup crumbled dried rosemary
  leaves

1 teaspoon white pepper
1 teaspoon ground ginger
⅛ cup whole celery seed
¼ cup crumbled dried marjoram
  leaves

Mix together thoroughly in blender.

MAKE YOUR OWN PIMIENTOS

Every year we allow a few of our green, sweet, bell peppers to ripen fully to a bright red. We use these several ways. We cut them up fine and freeze for garnish on casseroles, and make some into pimientos as follows: Wash peppers and remove seeds. Place on cookie sheet; put under broiler, turning as they brown, watching closely so as not to burn. When brown, skin them. Put peppers in jar and cover with either olive oil or vegetable oil. Soak for 2 or 3 days. Then remove from the oil and put in plastic bags in small amounts and freeze. Save oil for salad dressing.

DEVILED HAM

The devil it is in truth, since for a huge price you are given enough for two sandwiches in those teeny cans in the store. Herewith, we have adapted Mrs. Beeton's 1869 potted ham recipe. If you make it ahead and in quantity, it could provide for a whole summer's sandwiches. All that will be missing from the canned formula will be sodium nitrite, which is bad for you.

2 pounds lean ham
1 tablespoon brown sugar
¼ pound butter or margarine
1 teaspoon ground mace
½ teaspoon ground allspice

½ teaspoon ground nutmeg
2 tablespoons vinegar
Dash cayenne pepper
2 tablespoons dried onions

Cut ham in small chunks. Mix all ingredients and place half of mix in blender. Whirl until smooth; remove first amount and blend second half. Add first portion and mix all. If extra liquid is needed, use vegetable juices. Pack tightly in jars and refrigerate. Will keep for two weeks; or freeze in small containers.

LOW-CALORIE, LOW-COST SOUR CREAM

½ cup buttermilk   1 24-ounce carton cottage cheese

Put into blender (½ at a time) and whirl until smooth. It will be quite runny but will thicken in refrigerator. The sour cream will keep about 10 days.

Tips
To make sour milk, add 1½ tablespoons lemon juice to 1 cup milk.

To make French mustard, mix together thoroughly 1 teaspoon each of dry mustard and olive oil with enough vinegar to make nice and smooth.

OUR FAVORITE SWISS-STYLE CEREAL

1 cup blanched almonds
1 cup whole filberts
3 cups quick-cooking
   rolled oats
¾ cup wheat germ

1 cup currants
⅔ cup finely chopped
   dried apricots
¾ cup firmly packed brown sugar

Spread filberts and almonds on rimmed baking sheet. Bake at 350° for from 5 to 8 minutes or until lightly brown; shake pan occasionally. Cool and chop nuts. Blend all ingredients together, store at room temperature in tightly closed container. Serve with milk. Makes 8 cups.

CANDIED ORANGE, LIME, LEMON, GRAPEFRUIT PEEL

Scrape the white matter from the rind with a teaspoon; cut peel in long, narrow strips; drop into boiling water for 5 minutes. Drain and cool. Place peels in cold simple syrup (equal parts sugar and water boiled until sugar is completely dissolved; cool) for 24 hours. Drain, saving syrup. Bring syrup to a boil and add peels. Cook to 230° to 240° until it threads from the spoon. Cool. Repeat this process. Remove peel; place on waxed paper, separating the strips from each other. When cool enough to touch, roll each piece in granulated sugar. These make a delicious candy. Save syrup to use in puddings or cakes.

YOUR OWN SALTED ALMONDS

We always do our own salted nuts since they are fresher and less expensive. Shell 1 bag almonds. To blanch the almonds and remove skins, put almonds into fast-boiling water for about 3 minutes. Drain and press wide end of nut; almond will pop out of the pointed end.

Allow skinned almonds to dry for about 15 minutes. Put ½ cup olive oil and ½ cup salad oil (or all salad oil) in deep saucepan. Heat oil until a drop of water will sizzle in it. No hotter. Carefully slide almonds into oil. Stir with metal slotted spoon until nuts begin to turn very light brown. Remove pan from stove and take almonds out quickly with slotted spoon. Put on brown paper bag, opened flat, to drain, then shake in a paper bag with 1 teaspoon salt.

We also do pecans, filberts, and brazil nuts. We do not blanch these.

OVEN-ROASTED SOYBEANS

Soak 1 pound of soybeans overnight in 1 quart of water to which 2 teaspoons baking soda have been added. Boil 1 hour in the same water. Drain. Spread in shallow pan. Roast in 350° oven for 30 minutes. After 15 minutes, remove, stir in 2 tablespoons butter or margarine. Return to oven until brown. Sprinkle with salt.

FROM CIDER TO VINEGAR

If you have access to untreated cider (no sodium, no pasteurization) in the fall when roadside stands are brimming with apples and apple products, buy an extra gallon or two of fresh cider. Put them away in a dark, cool place. Forget about them for about six months. When you take them out, you will find a cloudy mass at the bottom of the jug. Don't worry: this was formed as part of the process of turning cider into vinegar. It is called the "mother." Pour off the clear vinegar into jars with coated tops. Besides being better flavored, this vinegar is a real economy. Vinegar bought in the store is heavily diluted with water; your vinegar is full strength, and if you wish, can be diluted with water as you use it in these proportions: ¾ cup home vinegar to ¼ cup water.

FRESH HORSERADISH

1 horseradish root (1 pound)
1 cup vinegar
1 teaspoon salt

1 teaspoon sugar
1 small potato, peeled and cubed

Scrub and peel horseradish, cutting away dark parts; cube. Place vinegar, salt, and sugar in blender. Add half each of horseradish and potato. Whirl until smooth. Add remaining horseradish and potato gradually.

Blend until vegetables are uniformly grated. Keep in refrigerator. Makes about 3 cups.

"CONFECTIONERS' " SUGAR

A working girl must do much of her holiday cooking at night. Desperation over cookies needing confectioners' sugar when the cupboard was bare of it led to this.

Place 1 cup of granulated sugar in blender, grind at medium speed for a few seconds, turn off blender, and, with a long spatula, stir sugar around. Grind at high speed until it reaches desired texture. If you wish to approximate commercial powdered sugar, add a rounded teaspoon of cornstarch to the cup of sugar before grinding. Measure for your recipe after grinding. We have also tried brown sugar this way. Since it is a wetter sugar than granulated, it will not grind as fine and fluffy, and the cornstarch really helps.

PRESERVING GINGER ROOT

Purchase the ginger root (or grow it). Take the weight of the ginger in sugar. Cover the ginger with boiling water and let cook rapidly till very tender. Dissolve the sugar in some of the water in which ginger was cooked. Use about ¼ as much water as sugar. Let cook to a thin syrup, skim, put in the ginger and let simmer very slowly till the syrup is nearly absorbed; then cook more quickly, stirring meanwhile to cause the sugar to grain until the ginger is well glazed. Or, remove the ginger from the syrup, drain, cut in strips, and roll in granulated sugar.

CATSUP

8 pounds chopped ripe tomatoes
4 onions, sliced

1 clove garlic
1 tablespoon salt

Cook till tender, then put in blender and add

¾ cup brown sugar
½ teaspoon allspice
¼ teaspoon cloves
Pinch ground cumin

Pinch ginger
¼ teaspoon oregano
¼ teaspoon black pepper

Simmer on low fire until ½ original amount. Stir often to prevent burning. Add 2 cups cider vinegar. Cook 10 minutes. Seal in jars.

YOUR
GARDEN

FLOWERS AND FRUITS ON YOUR TREE

If you are planning to plant a flowering tree in your landscape, why not pick one that will also produce fruit for you? Many fruit-bearing peach, plum, cherry, and apple trees are fully as beautiful as the purely decorative ones. The dwarf or semidwarf varieties produce earlier in life and are more in scale with residential plantings than full-sized trees. If you garden organically, many of the fruit diseases will not occur. There are also some new varieties which have disease resistance bred into them. You will have your ornamental, and fresh unsprayed fruit too. Armstrong Nurseries has two fine peach trees developed for both flowering and fruiting (see page 246).

ORNAMENTAL VEGETABLES

Consider planting some vegetables in your flower garden. Both hot and sweet peppers make handsome plants, and the ripening Hungarian wax pepper changes from green to yellow, to orange, to red as it ripens. One plant may simultaneously have all colors. The gray-green leaves, lavender flowers, and handsome fruit of the eggplant are decorative too. If your climate allows, try growing the globe artichoke. This larger-than-life lookalike of the thistles makes a foundation of gray-green leaves up to 2 feet long. Though you eat the buds before they flower, globe artichoke is a real foliage addition to your garden.

The Greeks had a word for it. Ecology and economy have roots in the Greek word, oikos, meaning house. Ecology, having to do with the environment—which is the house—and economy, the management of the house.

Tip

Don't let those leaves get away! To the organic gardener the sight of three to ten plastic bags of leaves left at the curbside for the city trash collector is totally revolting. Often, the gardener will stop and ask to have them, thus incurring a variety of reactions, often unstated, but felt all the same. Such as: "you interfering   , I can do what I want with my leaves," "Must be mighty poor, wants to sell them or something," "What good are leaves (or pine needles or...), they just ruin my lawn?" or "Sure take them, I don't want them." By packing leaves or pine needles in plastic bags for the trash pickup, you do the following:

Dispose of the best soil conditioner nature has. Deep, rich, productive soils are made of decayed plant and animal materials.

Fill our city trash dumps prematurely by delaying nature's natural decay process (the plastic bags).

Add chemicals of unknown danger to our soil and water (the plastic bags).

Spend your income on chemical fertilizers that never provide the nutrition that these wasted natural materials can.

EDIBLE GROUND COVER

We earlier mentioned New Zealand spinach as an edible ground cover. There are other ground covers which provide a green or blooming blanket and which can also contribute to your kitchen. Nasturtiums—the dwarf types—are excellent for a ground cover. Use the flowers to top a summer salad, the leaves in tossed salads and on open-faced sandwiches instead of watercress, and the seeds for capers. When seeds are ripe and fat, drop them into an open jar with salt in the bottom until you have some thoroughly dried. Pack these dried seeds (without salt) tightly in a jar of vinegar. Use as needed as caper substitute. Nasturtiums like full sun and do not need a rich soil. They will grow with less sun, but bloom less frequently.

Strawberries, with their almost evergreen foliage and early starry white blossoms, make an excellent bank cover since their habit is to send out runners to cover the bare ground. They should have a light, well-drained, rich soil in full sun to produce the maximum berries. They will, however, tolerate considerable shade. To avoid continuous quarreling with the birds over who owns the berries, purchase a one-crop variety. While the berries are ripening, you can cover the bank with inexpensive tobacco netting. The strawberry plant is handsome for shadier wooded locations; you can also use wintergreen or partridgeberry. Both are evergreen and have nutritious berries.

HOT AND PRETTY

Hot peppers are easy to grow. We have grown both Hungarian wax and cayenne long red thick. The former is best for fresh cooking and freezing, the cayenne best for drying. Hot pepper plants placed around the periphery of your garden will help hold down rabbit and deer damage. Evidently one bite of the leaves convinces the animals that there is nothing worth eating inside the "pepper fence." If your garden is of any size, this means lots of hot peppers, since the plants bear long and are prolific. Cayenne peppers can be hung to dry and used as needed. To quick-dry Hungarian wax peppers: slit peppers in half, remove seeds and pulp, lay seeds and skin on cookie sheet, and slip into turned-off oven after removing something you have cooked. Don't forget to remove them before you relight the oven. They produce an acrid smoke when burned. When thoroughly dry, whirl in the blender until desired fineness is realized. We use dry peppers in these ways: ground fine in recipes calling for cayenne peppers; as a substitute for Java pepper at the table (it's different but good); with ground cumin, garlic, and oregano for chili powder; ground very fine and added to water for an insect repellent spray. Remember to wear gloves when working with hot peppers.

INCREASING YOUR PLANTS

Have your own small plant nursery. Here is a way to increase your stock of ornamental woody plants and roses. Save your cans of all sizes; rinse thoroughly; remove paper wrapper. Punch three holes in the sides at the bottom with a beer can opener; drop a small piece of broken clay pot, brick, or even a porous stone into the bottom. Mix some garden soil half and half with sand and insert cutting after dipping bottom of stem in hormone powder according to directions. Using a flat plastic tray or a bucket, put the cans to soak up water through the holes in the bottom. After a few hours the topsoil will feel wet to the touch. Never top-water a new transplant or cutting in a can. Soaking through bottom holes will do it for you. When topsoil feels wet to the touch, remove cans and allow to drain. Pick a semishaded spot in the garden where they will not be an eyesore or disturbed. Stack cans close together and pull soil or leaves up around them so that the sides and rims are hidden. Forget about them, except in a prolonged dry spell when they could use some watering. After a few months check for new top growth. If new leaves are showing, the plant is starting roots. Plants can remain in the cans for up to a year and should not be set out in the garden sooner than four months after rooting for best results. When visiting friends, ask if you may take a cutting of a desired plant; be sure at least three nodes are on the cutting; slip it into a plastic bag to avoid its dehydrating until you get home. Trim off all but two or three leaves, dip in hormone powder, can, and you are all set with a new plant.

Tips

Some things are right in front of our noses and we do not see them. After my mother's home was sold, I missed the fruit from the quince tree from which we made our jelly. Just last year I was looking at the funny little fruits on our dwarf flowering quince bushes. I bit into one, and sure enough, it had a good quince flavor. We could make our favorite jelly again! I use the fruit pectin recipe, but cut down on the lemon juice called for, since we like a really strong quince flavor.

Of course we use ladybugs and praying mantises in our garden, but have you ever thought that they would do just as good a job of bad bug disposal in your plant window? The praying mantis dies after laying eggs, but ladybugs will not hibernate if they are in a warm house. They are a great help with scale insects, aphids, and white flies.

Plant chives or garlic close to your roses; aphids will stay away.

Citrus fruit peels are an excellent addition to your compost pile. They are high in phosphorus and also contribute potash and nitrogen.

A BOUNTIFUL BUSH

Robert Frost has celebrated the blueberry in a poem simply called "Blueberries." Andrew Wyeth's nostalgic "Distant Thunder" also celebrates the joy of picking these fine berries, in the wild. The march of "civilization" has placed wild blueberry picking out of the reach of many, but this does not mean that one must forswear the pleasure of picking and eating this easily grown berry. There are varieties of blueberry for almost every area of the United States, from Maine to California. The bushes can be grown on even the smallest property. They can be used to edge a driveway, as an ornamental hedge around a garden, or in a special plot by themselves. The medium-sized bushes are handsome at all times of the year, with showers of white flowers in spring. In the fall their leaves turn an attractive scarlet. In winter their branches and twigs make a graceful tracery. The sucessful culture of blueberries is dependent chiefly upon a soil which is acid and full of humus. Using leaves and compost, it is possible to make almost any soil into a suitable growing medium for blueberries. Two varieties must be planted for cross-pollination. This berry freezes and cans well, and is versatile in its cooking uses.

DELICIOUS DILL AND BASIL

Of all the herbs we grow, our two favorites are dill and sweet basil. Both are easy to grow; both are attractive in the flower garden. Here are some suggested uses:

Dill: A lovely, feathery plant with flat, yellow, Queen Anne's Lace-like flowers. We use fresh leaves and flowers cut up fine in a green or potato salad. We dry whole stalks when seeds mature, saving seeds and crumbling dry leaves for flavoring. We use the dried stalks in the fire when broiling fish on the grill or wrap in foil with the fish when baking.

More dill ways: sprinkle on green salad, on top of creamed vegetables or casseroles, on any fish and delicate meats such as veal and poultry. Cook a sprig with lima beans, green beans, or fresh peas.

Basil: There are two varieties of basil available. One is green; the other, called Dark Opal basil, is a handsome, dark, purplish-bronze color. Either basil is an easily grown plant the leaves of which are very useful in flavoring soups and stews, especially beef dishes. The leaves can be used fresh or dried. If using them fresh, exert caution in the amount.

FOR THAT BACK CORNER

You might try growing Jerusalem artichokes and horseradish in a back corner of your flower garden. The Jerusalem artichoke is related to the sunflower and looks like a yellow cosmo. Its roots are a good substitute for water chestnuts called for in Oriental dishes.

To prepare: Brush with a wire brush. Soak in salt water overnight, then slice thin to add to green beans or casseroles. Also slice thin and serve raw in salads. To add Jerusalem artichoke to a casserole or vegetable soup, cut into 1-inch cubes and sauté.

Horseradish can become quite a weed. But its roots are prized for their hot flavor in sauces. Roots may be purchased through most seed houses. They are best flavored when dug in autumn or winter. You can "put them down" in vinegar to preserve them or prepare to use as follows:

Grate horseradish after washing and peeling. Add a teaspoon of vinegar, pinch of sugar, salt, and pepper to taste.

Tip

If you use charcoal for outdoor cooking, instead of the marvelous Swanie-braai, save used charcoal. Break into small pieces and add to your compost. Only natural charcoal should be used this way.

STEALING A MARCH ON APRIL

To grow lettuce year round you can cover a small area in a sunny, wind-protected spot near the house very inexpensively using wire garden hoops and 4 mil clear plastic. Hoops ⅛ inch in diameter and 22 inches high are best. Placed about 2 feet apart they will support the plastic, but a gentle slope should be planned to provide automatic runoff for rain and melting snow. Long pipes or logs should be rolled at the bottom edge of the plastic to hold it taut. On warm sunny days the plastic can be rolled open and closed again in the late afternoon. At temperatures down to 0° F this system will keep plants from freezing. Radishes and fresh herbs may also be kept available all winter in this way. Cool-weather seedlings will start well in this low-cost greenhouse, and it can be removed when no longer needed.

MINICOMPOSTING

For many, the garden compost pile is impractical because of space limitations. Kitchen waste can be put to good use and fertile soil for plant growth can be made by following one of these methods:

Direct burying: Dig a hole in your garden about 2 feet deep and 2 feet wide. Place kitchen waste in it and add a small amount of soil each time until the hole is full. Stamp down and start again with an adjacent hole. Be sure to cover these holes with a large piece of plywood or other sheet material to keep dogs from digging.

Plastic garbage can: Place a 2-inch layer of soil in can: add kitchen wastes as available, each time covering with some soil. Sprinkle lightly with water. Keep covered.

Heavy-duty plastic bag: This is an efficient vessel for compost making. Located in a sunny spot, the black plastic will absorb heat and hasten the process. Disadvantage: dogs can tear it open. Use layering method described above. Fastened tightly closed, this bag can be turned over to mix the ingredients.

Small plastic bags: Even in an apartment, three strong freezer bags, one inside the other, will produce potting soil.

INGREDIENTS FOR COMPOSTING

Coffee and tea grounds, cut-up citrus peels and seeds, eggshells, banana skins, unusable vegetable parts (carrot tops, skins, potato peels, etc.), chicken and small beef bones. Add animal manure. Even dried cow manure will help. Never use animal fats in compost. Never flush your potential plant food down the disposal.

RECYCLING AND ENERGY SAVING

SOAP SAVING

Those annoying, thin, end-of-the-soap-bar bits can be saved and used in an old-fashioned soaper such as grandmother used at her kitchen sink. Hunt through flea markets and secondhand shops until you find one. A brisk whisking through a sinkful of warm water produces a good pan-rinsing liquid and saves on soap and pollution.

Tip

When we lived in New Hampshire, we had hot water radiant heat in our floors. I used to place eucalyptus leaves or garden herbs under the rugs for a nonaerosol-produced room fragrance. When we moved to North Carolina we had air heat and air conditioning. I was able to achieve the same effect with bunches of herbs over the duct grilles. These herbs should be changed about every month. It is pleasant to have a different fragrance in each room. Eucalyptus branches can be rinsed free of dust and will keep their fragrance with this treatment for months. This is a home use of herbs related to the use of "strowing" herbs in Colonial days.

WAYS WITH SALT

We buy the least expensive salt available and use it in many ways:

To debug garden vegetables (see page 86).

To clean burned pans: soak overnight with ¼ cup salt, 1 cup water, and a slice of onion. Next morning boil for 5 minutes and pour off. Your pan should be clean.

To clean copper-bottomed saucepans, dip a slice of lemon, or a half lemon after you've squeezed it, in salt and scrub.

To clean silverware: 1 tablespoon salt to 1 quart of water and 1 table-spoon bicarbonate of soda. Put silver into mixture and boil for 3 minutes in an aluminum pan. Wipe dry and rub with a soft cloth.

To keep away ants and cockroaches.

To use as gargle for sore throats: 1 teaspoon salt to 1 glass hot water.

To make into nose drops: ¼ teaspoon salt to 4 ounces of lukewarm water. Dissolve completely.

To use instead of scouring powder.

SOME COMMON REUSABLES

In order to achieve the fullest recycling possible within your home, think of the cost you pay to have the producer package those products you buy. When you are headed for the wastebasket with an empty container— STOP—is there some way to use it?

Use the composition cardboard trays upon which your supermarket fruits and vegetables rest in plasticized splendor for arranging a head of garden lettuce, a tomato, and some radishes for a gift to some elderly person who cannot garden.

Save the glass herb bottles with the punched plastic tops, plus screw-on lid. Dry any flower or vegetable seeds or herbs you wish to save. When you are sowing seeds, use this bottle to distribute them. They can be recycled to their original use to hold your own dried herbs.

We buy fresh fruit yogurt in the 8-ounce plastic cups and use the cups until they are worn out. They go through the dishwasher perfectly if placed in the top rack. We use them to measure one cup; to take coffee, tea, or lemonade out to the garden when we are working; to store mayonnaise, sour cream, or leftovers. We use them also with a hole punched in the bottom to pot up seedling plants.

Save mesh bags. We put to good use the orange or yellow plastic mesh bags that produce is sold in, and the coarser fiber mesh bags that hold potatoes or onions. We use the lightweight plastic bags for drying herbs; the coarser, bigger bags for our potato, turnip, onion, or winter squash crop. We hang these bags from a homemade rack in a cool, dark (but not damp) place and use the contents as needed.

Save those nice clean wads of cotton with which the manufacturer so frugally stuffs the top third of a bottle of aspirin or vitamin pills. Collect them in small clean plastic bags, seal with twist-tops, and you have ideal cosmetic wipes.

We cut up bleach bottles for plant markers. Remove the top curved portion first, then cut with strong scissors, down toward the bottom in width desired. After cutting these loose from the bottom, we taper one end. These take Magic Marker well and look trim in the garden.

Of course we also use cut bleach bottles to make funnels, boat bailers, and as floats to mark a boat mooring.

If your children have been through the tropical fish stage and you have an abandoned fish tank around your house, you have an ideal seed-starting or cutting rooting box. Add a piece of glass as a top (tape edges so they won't cut), and you have not only a possible terrarium, using gathered wildlings (from construction sites), but a way to prepare for your summer garden during the winter. Merely fill the bottom 3 inches with good soil and sand, half and half mix, sprinkle lightly, put the aquarium with seeds or cuttings in an east or southeast window, and watch it grow.

Keep all those clay pots. They are becoming rare and expensive as tin cans replace them in plant nurseries. A plant flourishes in a clay pot because the clay will take up and hold moisture and air through its pores, whereas a tin or plastic pot is merely a straitjacket for the plant. Remember, potter's clay is cooked earth.

Tip

To keep "skin" from forming on the top of a can of paint, lay a flat piece of Saran wrap on top of the paint.

RECYCLE, RECYCLE

There are many uses for waxed cardboard cartons our milk comes in. As oil scarcities and costs increase, plastics of all kinds will become rare and expensive—possibly a good thing in view of the problems with their disposal. (The cardboard cartons are, of course, coated with a petroleum product, but much less is used here than in an all-plastic bag, box, or bottle.)

Cut enough of the tops off cartons to make them pint size for starting seeds. Cut tops and bottoms from cartons and use the square "sleeves" remaining to protect young transplants from cutworms and slugs, rabbits and mice, sun and wind. Lift off or cut away after plants are well established.

The cartons can also be used to store vegetables and cold liquids in the freezer, and we use one carton to start a fire in the fireplace.

We had some Styrofoam trays with slip-on windowed covers left from some of our defunct miniature Christmas lights. These make excellent indoor seed-starting trays if the "window" is large enough. Remove cover when seeds show secondary leaves, or earlier if plants are touching the cover.

ABOUT BUYING IN QUANTITY

If you live in a region where citrus fruits cannot grow, try to find a farmers' market where you can buy by the box. We find grapefruit and lemons the best buys. Oranges don't keep as well and their quality seems spotty. We squeeze grapefruit for about a three days' supply of juice at one time. Quart jars capped tightly and refrigerated will maintain the vitamin C content. We always have a few in the refrigerator hydrator for eating in halves with honey instead of sugar. The rest of the box of grapefruit we keep in a cool place, and with occasional sorting, they will keep for three weeks, if we don't eat them before that. If you plan to bulk-buy and prepare store fruits and vegetables, call your state agriculture department for a list of the times of year when the things you wish to store are in greatest supply or in danger of being lost in storage. These times differ for different fruits and vegetables, and parts of the country. Because you must give storage space to them, you shouldl try to buy at the bottom price in order to make a saving. You may have to be fairly insistent to get this information, but it is available to you wherever you are.

We buy yeast, baking powder, oatmeal, and vanilla in bulk amounts from our favorite source—Walnut Acres (see Appendix, page 246). Though organically grown foods are usually more expensive than the chemically mass-produced variety, if you buy in quantity for your long-term needs, you will find that there are real savings here. The average city or suburb dweller will not be able to eliminate chemicals completely from his or her diet. However, he or she can cut down intake of these unknown hazards by "diluting" the diet with many organically grown components. In planning for your family, think constantly of the potential dilutions that you can arrange within your budget.

Tip

We use a lot of lemons in hot drinks and in cooking and salad dressing (lemon juice is a good substitute for vinegar). We squeeze half a box of lemons at one time. In an accumulation of ice cube trays, we freeze the juice into cubes. Remove from trays and bag. One-half cube makes a mug of hot lemonade. With a teaspoon of honey, this is a delicious, healthful drink. One cube makes a tall glass of lemonade. A melted cube instead of vinegar called for is used for a batch of salad dressing. Other uses: To add zip to the apples in a pie, to make your own lemon gelatin; 8 cubes = 1 cup lemon juice.

Tips

Warm a casserole on a stove burner by using your cast-iron Dutch oven. Place casserole on the trivet with about 1 inch of water in the bottom of the oven. Warm slowly.

From Housekeeping in Old Virginia (1879) come the following household hints:

"To remove egg stains from silver spoons. Rub with salt and it will entirely remove the discoloration produced by eating a boiled egg with a silver spoon. Rubbing with salt will also remove grayish streaks that collect on white tea-china." (See also page 232.)

"To prevent fruit stains from being permanent. Wet the stained spot with whiskey before sending it to wash, and there will be no sign of it when the article comes back."

"Borax. It is very desirable to keep borax in the house. Its effect is to soften the hardest water and it is excellent for cleaning the hair."

Tips

Use empty toothpaste tubes for small weights: fish line sinkers, etc.

A little dab of household ammonia will ease the hurt of an insect bite.

A very strong solution of borax will take brown stains off your casseroles.

To take out fruit stains, tie up cream of tartar in the spots and put the cloth in cold water, to boil, or, if stains are much spread, stir the cream of tartar into the water, boil and pour over stain.

To remove perspiration odor from synthetic fabrics, soak in baking soda water.

Clear boiling water will remove tea stains.

Borax will remove the yellowing on linen that has been stored.

Tips
We have found that a stem of fresh tansy will drive ants out of a kitchen cupboard. The plant grows 2 to 5 feet high and has feathery leaves useful in flower arranging. The yellow flowers are attractive too. It should be grown in good soil in full sun. You can grind the leaves with some water in your blender to make an ant repellent spray for peonies, etc.

A roach chaser which will not tempt your pets. Sprinkle borax at baseboards and on shelves.

Camphor instead of mothballs. We like the fragrance of camphor much better than the usual mothball odor. You can buy it in small blocks at the drugstore. It is every bit as effective.

Make you own furniture polish: 4 tablespoons sweet oil, 1 teaspoon lemon juice, 10 drops ammonia; mix thoroughly. (Sweet oil may be purchased at the drug store.)

Tips
"Banana skin for cleaning tan leather suitcases. Rub the leather well with

the inside of the skin, wipe off any excess moisture, finish with a good polishing with a dry cloth—it works!" (From The Boston Cooking School Magazine, August—September 1910.) Bananas have stayed remarkably low in price. They have excellent food value and their skins add important nutrients to the compost.

For cleaning windows, nothing works better than crumpled newspapers and plain ammonia. Do not get the kind labeled "sudsy" or one that says detergent added.

We have had the much advertised problem with "ring around the collar," especially on wash and wear shirts. After trying all of those expensive chemical mixes to little avail, we hit upon the perfect combination—ordinary laundry soap and elbow grease, the elbow grease via a small glass washboard, which we ordered from Cumberland General Store (see Appendix, page 246). The store has a fine catalog of just such hard-to-find items.

OLD RECIPES

A good old recipe for removing mildew from linen is to take 2 tablespoons of soft soap and the juice of a lemon. Lay it on the spots with a brush on both sides of the linen. Let it lie for a day or two until stain disappears.

If any material has been scorched and the mark has not penetrated entirely through so as to damage the texture, it may be removed by using this old recipe:

Peel and grate 2 onions and extract the juice. Add 2 tablespoons soap flakes and ½ pint vinegar. Mix and boil this composition well, then spread it when cool over the scorched part of material and let dry. Afterward, wash out the material and mark will have been removed.

A NEW USE FOR BALLOONS

"In Paris, it has been found practicable to dry clothes by means of stationary balloons. The large laundries that have them charge a little higher price for clothes thus dried above the soot of the city in pure air.

"The clothes are suspended on racks hung from the balloons.

"If our cities become much more crowded, with elevated roads, roof gardens, etc., as the only means of getting above the crowd, ere long families in apartments will be having a balloon nursery instead of sending infants out with nurses to the squares or parks in carriages.

"The household will not be hushed during nap time; baby will be sky-high. Instead of watching from the doorway to see if he is awakening, they will take a telescope to see." (From the Boston Cooking School Magazine, December 1899.)

USES FOR BAKING SODA

Baking soda is an excellent inexpensive tooth cleaner. Use it three or four times a week as a change from your expensive advertised brand. It is superior as a mouthwash and breath sweetener with a sprig of mint chewed afterward.

A solution of 1 teaspoon soda to ½ cup water, stirred well, will make a good deodorant.

Poison ivy sufferers are familiar with soda's soothing effects.

Food stains on kitchen counters can be removed with soda.

You can use a mild solution of baking soda and water to remove corrosion from the clamps and posts of your car battery. Make sure baking soda does not get into the cells. Use a wire brush for this.

Keep a box of baking soda near the stove at all times. In case of a grease fire, douse it with soda.

Keep a large box of baking soda in your car in case of a fire. For cleaning jewelry, use ½ teaspoon to 1 cup of water.

Tips

To clean spotted glassware, mix half and half vinegar and water. Wash, then dry with soft cloth.

Make your own inexpensive furniture polish. Mix ½ cup vinegar with ½ cup alcohol and 1 cup linseed oil.

A bit of butter at the tip of a pitcher spout prevents drips.

   Don't forget to use the cents-off coupons you find in your mailbox or in the newspaper. It is possible to save a great deal using these.
   However, use caution—be sure the product is one you use or one that you have been wanting to try. You may find the store's brands or a special sale might make other choices more economical.

For electricity saving when perking coffee on stove, allow pot to start to perk on high setting. As soon as it starts to perk, turn off burner; it will be done when it stops perking.

To make your Christmas tree more fire resistant, make a spray of 9 ounces of borax mixed with 4 ounces of boric acid in 4 quarts of water. cover tree thoroughly. Allow to dry before taking tree indoors.

We have always enjoyed using candles at dinnertime and for special occasions. Now, with the high electric costs, we have extended this to all light where reading is not done, except in bedrooms where we do not use candles because of the greater fire hazard.
   Candles are an additional fire hazard, and where there are small children they should be well out of reach or this economy should be foregone.

Whenever possible, heat water in your teakettle, then pour it over the food you are going to boil. Your teakettle is a more efficient utilizer of heat calories than a pan.

Here is an easy way to preserve eggs: Buy only farm-fresh eggs. At your hardware store, order ahead a pound of water glass. You may also be able to find the handsome pottery egg crocks in an old-fashioned hardware store. Wipe eggs with a soft cloth. Do not wash. Place eggs small end down in a large stoneware crock. Mix 1 pound water glass or liquid sodium silicate with 10 quarts of boiled water which has been cooled. Pour over eggs when solution is thoroughly cold. Be sure all eggs are covered. Eggs will keep for 3 to 4 months.

To clean your scorched coffeepot, use 1 tablespoon of baking soda and fill the pot with water to above the scorch line. Boil for a few minutes, empty, and repeat, leaving second boil to sit overnight. Rinse, and boil with clear water before using to make coffee.

It is possible to get a free bottle of salad oil in a year's time. When the bottle you are using is apparently empty, prop the bottle upside down with the mouth of the bottle sitting in a small dish. Leave it for a day, and reap your bonus. A 38-ounce bottle will give you ⅛ cup of oil which you might have thrown away.

THE MISTRESS

Strength and honour are her clothing; and she shall rejoice in time to come. She openeth her mouth with wisdom; and in her tongue is the law of kindness. She looketh well in the ways of her household, and eateth not the bread of idleness. Her children arise up, and call her blessed; her husband also, and he praiseth her.

Proverbs 31:25-28

OUR TABLE BLESSING

Back of the loaf the snowy flour, back of the flour the mill, back of the mill, the sun and the shower, the grain and our Father's will.

Source Unknown

Appendix

CHINESE VEGETABLE SEEDS
  Tsang and MA International
  PO Box 294
  Belmont, California 94002

DWARF FRUIT TREES
  Stark Bros. Nurseries
  Louisiana, Missouri 63353

FLOWERING AND FRUITING TREES
  Armstrong Nurseries, Inc.
  PO Box 437
  Ontario, California 91761

  Stark Bros. Nurseries
  Louisiana, Missouri 63353

GINGER AND OTHER TROPICAL
    PLANTS
  Alberts and Merkel
  2210 South Federal Highway
  Boynton Beach, Florida 33435

ORGANICALLY GROWN FOODSTUFFS
  Walnut Acres Mill Store
  Penns Creek, Pennsylvania 17862

SOLAR FOOD DRYER
  Western Botanicals Co.
  710 Wilshire Boulevard
  Santa Monica, California 90401

SWANIEBRAAI NEWSPAPER GRILLE
    (Quick-Cook)
  Heritage
  PO Box 30632, Crabtree Station
  Raleigh, North Carolina 27612

UNUSUAL SEEDS
  Meadowbrook Herb Farm
  Wyoming, Rhode Island 02989

  Nichols Garden Nursery
  1199 South Pacific
  Albany, Oregon 97321

WHITE MOUNTAIN ICE CREAM
    FREEZER, APPLE PARER,
    SOAPER, AND WASHBOARD
  Cumberland General Store
  Route 3, Box 479
  Crossville, Tennessee 38555

Cucumbers in a Flower Pot
   Alice Skelsky
   Workman Publishing Co.
   231 East Fifty-first Street
   New York, New York 10022

The Edible Ornamental Garden
   John Bryan and Coralie Castle,
      101 Productions
   834 Mission Street
   San Francisco, California 94103

Herb Cookery
   Alan Hooker, 101 Productions
   834 Mission Street
   San Francisco, California 94103

How to Grow Herbs
Sunset Guide to Organic Gardening
Sunset Vegetables Gardening
   Editors of Sunset Magazine
   Lane Magazine and Book Co.
   Menlo Park, California 94025

The Rodale Cookbook
   Rodale Press Book Division
   Emmaus, Pennsylvania 18049

The Rodale Herb Book
   Edited by William H. Hyltoh
   Rodale Press Book Division
   Emmaus, Pennsylvania 18049

Vegetarian Gourmet Cookery
   Alan Hooker, 101 Productions
   834 Mission Street
   San Francisco, California 94103

The Wok: A Chinese Cookbook
   Nitty-Gritty Productions
   PO Box 5457
   Concord, California 94524

SOME UNUSUAL MAGAZINES

The Mother Earth News
   105 Stoney Mountain Road
   Hendersonville, North Carolina
      28739

Organic Gardening and Farming
   33 East Minor Street
   Emmaus, Pennsylvania 18049

INDEX

MARGARET KING HUNTER was educated at Wheaton College and Harvard Graduate School of Design. She and her husband, Edgar H. Hunter, have had their own architectural firm, E. H. and M. K. Hunter, AIA, for thirty years. Their architectural practice started in New England and was moved to Raleigh, North Carolina, in 1966 where they now have their office. Mrs. Hunter also owns Heritage Antiques.

VIRGINIA W. WILLIAMS joined the Hunters in Raleigh in 1970 as assistant with Heritage Antiques until her death in 1976. Her special antique interest was in cookbooks published before 1900.

EDGAR H. HUNTER, the illustrator, was educated at Deerfield Academy, Darmouth College, and Harvard School of Design. A member of the Olympic Ski Team in 1936, he designed ski posters for Dartmouth College Carnival and the State of New Hampshire. He taught architectural design at Dartmouth College for the twenty-one years he practiced architecture in New England.

The Hunter family live on five acres with a one-acre pond and are using their land to develop systems for solar energy uses and subsistence organic gardening methods which can be adapted by the average homeowner.